DEATH IS NOT GOODBYE

CONNECT WITH YOUR LOVED ONES AGAIN

KIM WEAVER

ISBN: 978-19-5-036751-1

Published by

 LIFESTYLE
ENTREPRENEURS
P R E S S

If you are interested in publishing through Lifestyle Entrepreneurs
Press, write to: *Publishing@LifestyleEntrepreneursPress.com*

Publications or foreign rights acquisition of our catalog books.
Learn More: *www.LifestyleEntrepreneursPress.com*

Printed in the USA

50%
OFF

IN APPRECIATION FOR
YOUR PURCHASE

https://KimWeaverEvidentialMediumConsultation.as.me/
ENTER CODE - CONNECTED

Advance Praise

"After reading *Death Is Not Goodbye*, I now have practical tools in connecting with my loved ones that have passed. I love the way Kim Weaver provides the reader with stories to teach us how to connect with the spirit world in a way I could totally understand. This book has changed my life in how I connect with my spirit, the spirit world, and how I approach synchronicities in my life. Kim Weaver provided me with the guidance to understand how the death of my husband guides me in my current life. She has helped me put my life into perspective."

—Kendra Lindloff, MSN, RN

"*Death Is Not Goodbye* has given me the tools to start my own process to reach out to my loved ones on the other side and to make it a daily on-going conversation with my spirit guides. What I liked most about the book is sincere honesty and the love to help others understand the other side in a completely different way of what the old school taught. This book makes it now possible for me to do this without fearing the spirit world but to love it and listen. This book is a must for beginners."

—Randy Weigandt, key account manager

"This is one of the best books I have ever read about communicating with the spirit world. It was full of information that was fascinating and easy to understand. One thing I liked about the book was how the author dispelled some myths about communicating with spirit. The stories she told about her life and the readings she has done made me want to keep reading."

—Shari Bral, client/widow

"*Death Is Not Goodbye* is fascinating to read, full of honest heart-warming true stories. Kim Weaver helps one to understand what a medium is, how we all have spirit guides, and the best way to connect to our guides. Connecting to our guides also helps us connect to our dearly departed love ones. Kim has always gone the extra mile for her clients. She has a compassionate, caring soul for all humans. It is a joy to work beside Kim and see how she changes the lives of those still living."

—Marilyn Bernardo, administrative assistant

"What a wonderful book. This book will help you learn to connect with your loved ones that have crossed over by giving you a great foundation for future growth. I will recommend this book to my clients. as I feel this will help them to understand and grow spirituality."

—Shimen Averhoff, founder of Sacred Designs by Spirit

"A quick, accessible read on a potentially taboo subject. Kim writes in an encouraging, yet matter-of-fact manner, with a sense of humor. *Death Is Not Goodbye* is the 'how-to' of reconnecting with loved ones who are no longer with us. A must-read for grieving family members looking for answers, Kim gives the reader the step-by-step process of how to recognize what the departed are saying to us. This book may be just the right gift for friends and family members who are struggling to make sense of life after the profound loss of a loved one."

—Lisa Hish, client/widow

For those who have lost a loved one. May your loved ones in spirit find a way to reconnect with you so your hearts are forever healed with love. And to my spirit friends who have guided me, pushed me, and believed in me. Thank you, you are my lighthouse shining your light on my path. You are forever in my heart. Until we meet again friends, namaste.

Contents

Chapter 1:

Love Never Dies

*"You may be gone from my sight, but
you are never gone from my heart."*

—Author Unknown

Carol grew up in a small community in Iowa. Her family consisted of her mother, father, and two siblings. Her parents
have been an important part of the family dynamics her entire
life. Recently, they celebrated their fiftieth wedding anniversary.
Family has remained a constant and loving force in Carol's life.
She often spoke to both her parents via telephone. They still
have a landline like so many of their neighbors. Life was simple
where Carol grew up.

Her childhood included studying and learning about the
Lutheran faith. She was baptized and confirmed in her childhood
church. It was the only church she ever attended until she left
for college. She participated in Bible School in the summer and
sang in the church choir as a child and later as a teenager with
the adult choir. Her entire family, including her grandparents,
all attended the same church.

After her high school graduation, Carol attended a university
in Iowa and successfully completed her bachelor's and master's
degrees in Spanish. She felt fortunate to secure a job with an

Iowa governmental agency quickly after college. She was happy, and life was good. She landed a job in a career field that she was able to use her Spanish in. She always had a strong desire of wanting to help people and her job gave her much satisfaction in accomplishing that dream.

Shortly after college graduation and starting her first job she found a Lutheran church close to her new home and started attending. She was devoted to her church. She sang in the choir, volunteered whenever volunteers were needed, and she attended Bible study. She had developed a strong faith over the years.

A year after college, Carol met Brian. He was four years her senior. They had an instant attraction. Brian made her laugh and brought joy to her life. Carol had a tendency to take life a bit too seriously, and she was a worrywart. Brian was the exact opposite. He had a zest for life and met life head-on, enjoying every moment. Three months after their first date, they moved in together. Five years later, they married.

Carol and Brian were extremely happy the first four years. They loved each other and often discussed starting a family. Having a family was always in the plans as they both had loving families and fond childhood memories.

One day, Brian started experiencing breathing difficulties. He went to the doctor and was prescribed medication and sent home. Later in the evening, he started having severe breathing problems. He could not catch his breath. He asked Carol to take him to the emergency room. She was frantic and drove as fast as she could to the hospital. When they arrived at the hospital, Brian was immediately admitted.

While Brian was in the emergency room, Carol asked if she should call his parents. Brian was adamant in his response. He

KIM WEAVER

did not want anyone to know he was in the emergency room. Carol would later tell me that was just like him. He never wanted anyone to worry about him or go out of their way for him. But that night was different. Carol was sick with worry. While the doctor and medical staff were attending to Brian, she secretly called her parents to let them know what was going on. There was little they could do other than offer their support as they lived two hours away. Carol felt a little better just voicing her concern to them.

After approximately an hour in the emergency room, Brian was moved to a hospital room for observation. He had been in a regular hospital room for a little over an hour when he needed to use the restroom. The nurse asked if he would like to use a urinal or walk to the restroom. Brian told the nurse he did not want a urinal. The nurse left the room and Carol helped her husband out of bed and walk to the restroom. She waited and then helped Brian walk back to his bed.

Brian no more than sat on the side of the bed when he looked at Carol and said, "Please, help me." She lay him back on the pillow and he started turning blue. She ran into the hallway to get a nurse. The nurse entered the room and quickly rang the button indicating an emergency. Carol was escorted into the hallway. After a few minutes, the nurse reappeared into the hallway and asked Carol if she had called their families. Carol looked in the hospital room and could see the medical staff working on her husband. But all that kept going through her mind was what Brian had said. "Don't call my family." She then thought of seeing this scene play out several times in the movies. Eventually, they would get his heart beating again she thought. The nurse quickly turned and reentered Brian's hospital room.

3

Carol was unable to think clearly. The only person she could think to call without breaking her promise to Brian was the church choir director who Carol knew would be at the church that evening for choir rehearsal. When the choir director answered the phone, she informed Carol she was home sick and would call and send someone else from the church to the hospital.

A short time later, the nurse stepped into the hallway to speak to Carol again. The nurse stated it had been thirty minutes since they began working on Brian attempting to get his heart beating. The nurse asked Carol what she would like for the medical staff to do. The nurse also asked if she would like to see her husband. Carol replied yes and entered Brian's hospital room. Brian was lying on the bed with a doctor sitting on his stomach giving him CPR. Carol looked at everyone and stated, "You can stop now."

It was surreal to her. Everything happened in slow motion. She felt numb, and she had just instructed the medical staff to stop trying to save her husband. She wanted to die herself. Her husband had complained about not being able to breathe, and suddenly she couldn't breathe either. She waited for a moment as the doctor removed himself off of Brian's stomach. She walked over to the bed where Brian laid, picked up his hand, and said goodbye. Carol had just watched life exit the body of the man she loved. She couldn't help Brian when he begged for her help even though he was already in the hospital with all the technology available. She remembered feeling such agony.

When she left the hospital room and entered the hallway, she was greeted by familiar faces from her church. The choir director had been able to reach someone at the church, and they brought others for support. Carol looked at all of them and said, "Brian is gone." Then she had the painful task of calling Brian's parents. She first spoke with his mother and then Brian's father. All she remembered was his mother's sobbing and the dead silence of his father. She told them several times she was sorry. She knew from her own agony that nothing she would have said to them would take away their pain. They had just lost their only child.

In that one moment, everything changed. Life was different for Carol. The only thing constant in her life was her job and her church. She was extremely grateful for both. Coworkers and church members checked on her often the first month after Brian passed away. But as time passed, so did the visits and telephone calls. Eventually, she found herself alone. The pain she felt was unbearable. She was a thirty-eight-year-old widow, something she had never imagined would happen to her.

She tried spending time with her friends, but they were all married and she felt like a third wheel. Besides, she had tried talking to them, but they couldn't understand the loss of a spouse. There was no way she could make them understand her situation. Brian's family was a reminder of the constant pain, and her family lived too far away. She didn't want to go out in public. She didn't want to go anywhere alone. She went to work, attended church and church activities, and sat at home.

Carol never knew much about afterlife spirit communication. One day, a friend explained to Carol that she had some psychic abilities and went on to explain she received a message from Brian. Carol's friend told her she was only able to get bits and pieces of what Brian tried to say, but she did tell Carol that Brian was still with her, and everything would be okay. That conversation opened Carol's eyes to the possibility of afterlife communication.

Over the next few days, Carol thought back to some strange occurrences that happened in her home. She considered it strange at the time but never gave it another thought until her friend brought up Brian and the afterlife. Then it got her thinking. Was it possible? Did Brian cause the strange occurrences?

Carol immediately went on the internet and purchased books about afterlife communication. She read and studied to learn all she could about the subject. She watched well-known mediums in action, and after a few months, she booked a reading with a medium over the telephone. She was willing to do just about anything to connect with Brian one more time.

Her friend who gave her the first signs of hope regarding spirit communication from Brian told her about metaphysical fairs and expos. She invited Carol to attend a fair in Iowa City, but something came up, and Carol could not make it. Her friend then told her about the next fair coming to Des Moines. Carol marked it on her calendar and planned to attend.

It was at that fair I met Carol. It was in June of 2015 at the Iowa Metaphysical Fair. She signed up for a reading with me. I could tell she was nervous and anxious. Tears came to her eyes before I even began. I knew it was an important moment for her. She had been waiting and anticipating this for some time. She had already had one telephone reading, but this was different. This was in person, and this was the first time Carol had a one-on-one reading.

As an empath, I sensed her fears. Carol was in emotional agony that only others who have walked the same path can ever understand. She sat patiently and waited for me to begin. She was there hoping to hear from her deceased husband one more time. Her decision to do this was going against her entire church

6

belief system from childhood, yet she didn't care. Her love for her husband superseded all of that. She risked being exposed and feeling vulnerable all for the love of Brian.

As I began the reading, tears streamed down Carol's face. I felt the love from Brian. I even had tears as well. Brian confirmed his identity by providing pieces of information that only he could. Carol knew beyond a shadow of a doubt it was him. We hugged at the end of the reading. A month later, I heard from Carol again. She wanted to set up another appointment for a reading.

Over the next couple of years, Carol learned to see the signs sent from Brian. We had several readings, and I consider her a friend. Brian has helped by providing insight and information that validates it was him. In one reading, he even spoke Spanish to her, but I could only relay a word or two. My Spanish skills are less than adequate.

Carol continued attending church, singing in the church choir, and keeping the readings a secret from her friends and family. She believed in afterlife communication but was unsure how her family and church friends would react and feel about it. She wasn't sure they would accept it. She continued reading and studying about learning to connect with her husband in the afterlife. I received so much joy in watching Carol grow. She would see the signs and send me a message about them.

Approximately three years after Brian passed away, Carol met Daryl. I remember the day she sent me a message and asked, "Is it possible to have two soulmates in one lifetime?" Shortly after that question, Carol booked a reading. Since his passing, Brian had been instrumental in helping his wife to heal, continually giving her signs. Carol asked me if I thought she and Daryl would become a couple. Brian indicated to me it was not meant to be. I knew exactly what he was talking about. Daryl also had limited time left. I chose not to share that specific information with Carol that day.

I encouraged Carol to live each day as if it were heaven on earth, to enjoy Daryl's company, and to give gratitude to spirit for bringing him into her life. I told her the universe has a way of making things right, especially in our times of need. Daryl was a gift. I was happy for her. They spent time together, and his faith, like hers, was unshakable. He told her he had no fear of death and believed he was going to a much happier place when he died. Carol never shared with him her readings with me. She wasn't sure how he would feel about it.

Six months later, Carol informed me Daryl had cancer. He did not have much time left. She cried. I asked my spirit friends how a person could go through such suffering again. I didn't understand the point. My heart ached for Carol.

Daryl passed away a couple of months later. I felt so much compassion for Carol. In the end, it was Carol who helped me see and accept death even more than I realized. I was surprised at how peacefully Carol accepted everything. She was sad, and she felt grief. But this time she started looking for the signs immediately. The signs showed up, and she smiled. She knew Brian and Daryl were together. She received signs from them both from the start, within hours of Daryl's passing.

I recently had a reading with Carol. She has lived a life that few of us ever will to lose her husband at the age of thirty-eight, to feel as if you could not help him when that was his last dying request, and then a few years later, to meet another love of your life only to lose him as well is heart-wrenching to say the least. Carol is an inspiration to me. She has gone to hell and back. Her saving grace was that she can connect and see the signs from both her soulmates. She is at peace because she can communicate with them. And now her life goes forward with a smile and the knowledge that love never dies.

Carol's story is one of heartbreak and triumph. She has experienced the deepest heartache of all, yet she has learned to see the signs confirming her loved ones are still present and continue to interact with her from the afterlife. Carol has worked hard and put in the effort to develop her spiritual gifts. She is now confident in her ability to recognize the signs. It brings her a sense of peace that she can connect herself.

While I have experienced the emotional pain of losing someone close, I also feel extremely fortunate to see the signs of my loved ones just like Carol does. It has always been my dream to help others see beyond their own limiting beliefs in order to connect with their loved ones once more. Those in the afterlife feel the loss as well. Your loved ones love you and want to connect again.

After years of conducting readings, I developed a process for discerning afterlife communication. I saw specific steps and spiritual blocks that kept others from connecting to their loved ones. It has become my ultimate goal and mission to help as many people as possible to learn this process.

Over the past two years, I have mentored and coached several people to develop their own gifts of mediumship. Carol is one of many who have learned how their loved ones communicate with them. It gives me much joy when I receive a message from my students explaining in detail their most recent sign from the other side. They are so excited. What they have all learned is the simple truth: Death is not goodbye.

Chapter 2:

Destiny Awaits

"I refuse to run or hide from my
soul's calling no matter how difficult,
scary or extraordinary it may be. I
step up and accept my destiny."

—Lonerwolf

As a child, I encountered spirit visitors often. And to be honest, they scared the hell out of me. I had no idea why they were there or what they wanted from me. I prayed they would leave me alone. I had a nightly ritual for approximately two years. Every night, I opened my closet doors and pushed all my clothes to one side. I wanted to see if I could catch how my visitors entered my room. Next, I checked under my bed. Then I would turn the lights out and run and jump in bed just in case they snuck in under my bed. I didn't want them to grab my feet. For some reason, I thought if I pulled the bed covers up over my head, they couldn't penetrate the covers. But even doing that, I could still sense them, and I knew they were still there. It gave me anxiety.

Eventually, I had the courage to face what I sensed. I began asking questions, and surprisingly, I received an answer that was conveyed through my mind. The information was being sent telepathically. Finding the courage to face my visitors that one day changed my entire life. The visitors who once scared me were slowly becoming my friends. I had conversations in my mind with them.

Childhood

From a young age, I wondered why I was here and what my purpose was. This life never felt right to me. I often daydreamed of another life. I wondered what it was like in heaven. Even though I had a voice in my head telepathically communicating, I still second-guessed everything. I wondered if I understood the random thoughts correctly. It wasn't an actual voice in my head. It was more like a thought process. For example, if I said I'm going to the grocery store, I wouldn't need to explain every detail of how I was getting there. I would just automatically know what was included with the entire thought. I was working hard to learn the language. What made it more difficult was the fact it wasn't a constant thought process. It would come and go randomly.

I grew up on an acreage in rural Iowa. My family consisted of five people. I have two sisters, one older sister and one younger sister. My younger sister was adopted from Korea when she was fourteen months old. My father was instrumental in adopting my sister. He grew up in an orphanage and later became a foster child at the age of thirteen. My parents both worked full-time jobs, so my sisters and I spent time at a babysitter when we were young and by ourselves when we were old enough.

My family attended First Lutheran Church. I was baptized and confirmed there. Sitting in confirmation classes was difficult for me. I enjoyed my pastor, but my friends in spirit were not so thrilled with the information he was teaching at times. I was nudged to question him on the information and rules of the Lutheran Church. Because of that, I questioned my entire belief system and everything taught by the church. The overall message was awesome. It was man's ideas and rules that created problems in religion that bothered me.

Grandma's Validation

I was thirteen years old when my grandmother was diagnosed with cancer. She was given six weeks to live. I was devastated. She was the first person I had a close relationship with who was dying. One day when I visited her in the hospital, I asked her straight out if she was afraid to die and if she believed in heaven. She told me she wasn't sure, but she hoped there was a heaven.

For the next few weeks, we spoke candidly about life and death. Up until her diagnosed illness, death and the afterlife were subjects I kept to myself. I tried to talk to my family about my nightly visitors. No one wanted to talk about them or anything else about my experiences. I always wondered if the thoughts in my head were coming from heaven. I knew if I talked about it, people would label me crazy. My family did not want to hear it, so why would anyone else? But for some reason, I felt compelled to discuss it with my grandma before she died. It felt safe. I would quickly find out the importance of our conversations.

A few weeks later, on a Saturday, I was to attend a swim meet in a town an hour away from home. I woke up and told my mom I was not going to the swim meet. I told her I was going to go visit grandma in the hospital because I knew she was going to die that day. My mother explained to me I had made a commitment and an obligation to my other teammates. It was the district swim meet, and others would be counting on me. She then told me grandma would be fine. I reluctantly attended the swim meet.

While at the swim meet, I received a telephone call. I was informed of my grandma's passing. I was told that someone would be arriving at the swim meet to drive me home. The ride home was agonizing. I wished I had stuck to my desires and stayed home and visited her before she died. I had so many thoughts racing through my head. I wondered how I knew she was dying that day?

Upon arriving at the hospital my mother, father, my two aunts, and uncles were all standing in the hall outside my grand-mother's hospital room. They had been awaiting my arrival. It had been important I see her. My grandmother had requested that I see her after she passed. I had no idea of that request until that moment when my mom told me.

I entered my grandma's hospital room first. My mom and two aunts walked into the room directly behind me. I slowly walked up to my grandma's side and looked at her. She had the biggest smile on her face. My mom and aunts were in shock. No one had entered her hospital room since she had passed away my mother stated. My family had instructed the hospital staff that nothing was to be done with her body until I arrived and saw her. They were all extremely surprised. My mom said, "I wonder what her smile means?" I knew right away. I said, "She is telling me there is a heaven, and I am not crazy." It was a bittersweet ending. I lost my grandma. But she had also gifted me peace, clarity, and understanding in her death.

My mother was never the same after losing her mother. Family life was never the same. People say their families are dysfunctional. Well, mine comes with a capital "D." I worked so hard for my mother to love me my entire life. I excelled at sports, lettering fourteen times in four years. My mother never attended one single game. I was nearly a straight-A student, and I was responsible, worked a job and earned money. I just wanted to be loved. Nothing I did worked. Looking back, I can see how losing someone affects a person. I learned that lesson myself.

Marriage

I married my high school sweetheart three months after high school graduation. We attended a community college, earned our degrees, and moved to Texas upon graduation. He was a great guy. But I was restless, and I was nowhere near mature enough to be married. Our marriage ended after three years.

I went from the frying pan into the fire and quickly fell in love again. Two years later, I married my second husband. When I say frying pan into the fire, that would be literally. My life was turned upside down. I went from being responsible to wild child. My second husband introduced me to a lifestyle that was carefree. I experimented with just about every drug known and tasted about every alcohol produced. I always remained responsible when it came to working and paying the bills, though. One of us in the marriage had to.

The Beginning of the End

My second marriage was a rollercoaster. On Friday, December 13, I was devastated to learn my second husband was having an affair. He told me he cared for her and was sorry. That day was heart-wrenching. I found myself alone in Dallas, Texas. I was so far from home. I had just returned from Iowa after spending Thanksgiving with family, and I spent Christmas in Texas alone. I immediately applied for a part-time job to occupy my free time. Within a few days, I worked lots of hours.

A month later, on Saturday, January 11, 1986, I planned to attend a concert at Billy Bob's in Fort Worth, Texas with my two girlfriends Tonya and Bea. It was the first night since separating from my husband that I was going out for fun with the girls. All day, I had an uneasy feeling. I couldn't make sense of it until late afternoon. I had the same feeling I did the morning I knew my grandmother was going to pass away. Only this time, the feeling I had was connected to my father.

I frantically called my father. In those days, cell phones did not exist. There were only landlines. My parents had divorced three years earlier. My father meant everything to me growing up. He was the only one aside from my grandma I felt loved me for me with no judgment or expectations, always encouraging me. We were close, but since moving to Texas, I rarely spoke to him. I had last seen him a few weeks earlier when I had been home for Thanksgiving.

I attempted numerous times to call his telephone number but always got a busy signal. After several attempts, Tonya and Bea encouraged me to go enjoy the concert and call him on Sunday. I agreed and the three of us left for the concert. We watched the concert and then drove the hour back to my apartment. Upon arriving at my apartment, my older sister who had moved to Texas shortly after I did was waiting at my apartment. She said, "Dad was killed in an accident tonight. Get your things. We are driving home."

I was in shock. I was drunk. I wanted to scream at the top of my lungs like an animal in pain. I could barely stand. I just looked at my sister and said, "How was he killed?" She said, "In a plumbing accident." I couldn't think straight. I kept thinking, a plumbing accident? I then said to my sister, "I can't go with you. I have responsibilities with two jobs. I need to notify them both. I need to pack." But what I wanted to do at that exact moment was to die myself. I knew this was coming hours earlier, and yet I gave up calling my dad to attend a concert? How could I?

Tonya and I worked together at my full-time job. She had called my boss to tell him the news without me knowing. Early Sunday morning, my boss arrived at my apartment with a round trip plane ticket for home. He told me the flight was early evening and to take the next week off. So, I packed my bags, and Tonya drove me to the airport later that afternoon. Everything about that day was a blur.

I remember the flight was nearly empty. The poor older gentleman sitting in my row and the stewardess were attempting to console me as I cried like a baby the entire flight. Silent, uncontrollable sobs. Nothing and no one could help me. I just wanted the pain to end.

The next week continued to be a blur. But as I write this, I remember every detail as if it happened yesterday. Since my mother and father were divorced, I unexpectedly found myself in charge of my father's estate at the age of twenty-three

– something I never imagined. During that week, I took care of estate items as well as his funeral arrangements. My sisters were a big help. They were a blessing.

During the week I was home in Iowa attending my father's funeral, my husband called every day to check on me. When I arrived back home, he was at our apartment apologizing for everything he put me through. I'm sure it was a matter of him taking pity on me for my circumstances. And to be honest, I needed a shoulder to cry on. A little over a week after my father's funeral, I sat and watched the Challenger space shuttle explode. All I could think of was those poor families and the heart-wrenching pain they were feeling. I could relate to their thoughts and emotions. It so touched my heart.

I no more than got settled into my normal schedule when a month after my father's passing, I received a telephone call at work. My father's mother had passed away. My grandma was my father's foster mother. My grandparents had never legally adopted my father, but they had considered him one of their children. At my father's funeral, my grandmother sat next to his casket and wept. All she kept saying was, "My baby." My father visited his foster parents more than any of their five biological children except one. Once again, I found myself returning home to attend a funeral.

Again, I returned to Dallas a few days later and attempted to have a normal life. A month later, I returned home again. This time for my grandfather's funeral. My father's foster father. In approximately three months, I buried three people. I was beyond depressed by this time. I was in trouble emotionally and mentally. My weight dropped to eighty-five pounds. I was wearing girls' size fourteen clothing. I was averaging two hours

18

of sleep a night. Thank God for my older sister. She came to my apartment one day and said, "Either you go see a doctor, or I am taking you." She knew I was in trouble.

I did eventually come out of it but never fully recovered. I didn't care if I lived or died. My husband began seeing the other woman again, and drugs and alcohol became my constant companions. My life was a mess. Even when my husband and I were together, the marriage included way too many substances that were having a negative influence on my life.

Help Arrives

One Saturday, I dropped down to my knees and said to God, "I can't live like this. Please help me." That night I had a dream. In that dream, I was at a family reunion at my grandma's house who had passed away when I was thirteen years old. In my dream, the telephone rang, and someone answered it and said, "Kim, it's for you." I answered the telephone, and on the other end was my grandma. She said, "Kimmie, this is grandma. If you don't change your ways, you will be joining me here." My grandma was the only one that ever called me Kimmie. That was my validation the dream was real. The next day was the end of my drug use. Never touched anything again. I rarely drank alcohol from that point on. That dream was an awakening for me.

Because of all my drug and alcohol use, I no longer could hear my spirit friends. I had lost the connection. But within a week of that dream and lifestyle change, everything started to return. My thoughts became clear again. My husband and I lived in the same house, but we had become nothing more than roommates. Within a few months, we parted ways. We had not had an actual marriage for over a year. In all honesty, we should have never married.

I can see how everything happens for a reason. Soon after my second marriage ended, I moved home to Iowa. I reconnected with my first love. We married and had two children together. He also had two children from a previous marriage in which he had primary custody. We will soon be celebrating our thirtieth wedding anniversary. I could have saved myself a whole lot of heartache if we had just gotten married from the start, but then I would not have learned what I needed to in order to help others. I do believe my husband entered my life in divine timing. I love him with all my heart, and I feel loved by him as well. There is no doubt he is my soulmate.

Spiritual Experiences

I quickly began having spiritual experiences. I had more and more communication with the other side and visitors were starting to show up everywhere I went. I would sense them in the grocery store or at the post office. I would see a live person and next to them I would see a dead person. It was unnerving. I started thinking I was losing my mind. Perhaps I had fried all the remaining brain cells with my past experimentations. I was in dire need of answers.

At that time, we owned a lake home. It was peaceful. I loved to sit on the deck, close my eyes, and take in the serenity of it all. I had been questioning the other side for some time if I was going crazy. I wanted to know if I was making all this crap up. It wasn't like I wanted to see a doctor or even tell my husband. He probably would have never left the kids alone with me again. One night at the lake, I went to bed and said to the spirit world, "I need to know I'm not crazy and this is real." I then went to sleep.

Later that evening, I woke up and looked at the digital clock sitting on the dresser in the bedroom. The time read 12:00 a.m. I lay back down and fell back asleep. I awoke again and looked at the clock. The time read 1:00 a.m. I lay back down and drifted off to sleep. Soon I awoke again and read the clock. This time the clock read 2:00 a.m. This continued to 3:00 a.m., 4:00 a.m., and 5:00 a.m. At 5:00 a.m. I said to my spirit friends, "I believe you. Please let me sleep."

My Destiny

This clock experience sent my mind racing. I thought back to when I first moved to Texas and worked with a woman by the name of Gail. She read Tarot cards and invited me to a card reading party. I attended and she read my cards. She looked at me and exclaimed, "You're a medium." I looked at her and said, "No I'm not." That was the first time I ever had a card reading.

A year after my card reading with Gail, I changed jobs. There was a gentleman I worked with that was an astrologer. He asked if he could do my natal chart. I agreed as I knew nothing about a natal chart and even wondered how water was involved. Jim presented me with my natal chart reading and pointed to certain planets and houses. He looked at me and said, "You're a psychic medium." I looked at him and said, "No, I'm not." He laughed and said, "You cannot change your destiny."

A year after my astrology reading with Jim, I was promoted and moved to a different department. In that department, I met a young man named Mark. He was a numerologist and wanted to, you guessed it, read my numerology report. I agreed, and within a week Mark was telling me what I had already heard twice before. All I said to Mark was, "No, I'm not. I sell insurance."

Mrs. Odgaard – Sixth Grade

After the clock incident, the thought also occurred to me about a note I had received the week prior from my sixth-grade teacher. Mrs. Odgaard wrote, "Dear Kim, As I was unenthusiastically "sorting and heaving" the other day I found these pieces you had written in middle school. I had been impressed enough to save them and I am still impressed enough to send them to you. Do you ever write your thoughts for remembering? You should. Enjoy. Keep smiling. Helen Odgaard." The following was a poem I had written in sixth grade.

Dreams

My soul drifts to a land of dreams
as sleep begins to fall.

My mind is filled with thoughts
of things I never can recall.

And all the things that can't be
true in hours of daylight.

Are here for me to touch and feel
with simple, pure delight.

But then the day comes bouncing
back and all the dreams are gone,

And everything is real again with
wars and hate and wrong.

Just reading what I had written forty years earlier while I was in sixth grade was a big aha. I wondered why she kept my poems. She had taught school for forty plus years herself. She had read lots and lots of poems. And I wondered if there was some larger energy at play. The timing occurring at the same time as the clock incident was just weird to me. I reread my poetry countless times. How did I know back then that our world is so messed up? More questions than answers. The search was on.

My First Mediumship Reading

The first reading I conducted was for my girlfriend. Her father had passed away a few years earlier and there was a family issue with her mother and money. Her father was straight to the point and conveyed such clear thoughts. I shared her father's thoughts with her. I will never forget the look on her face. She said, "Oh my God, that is him. You need to do this. You are a medium." I thought, "Yeah, I have heard that before," and giggled to myself.

Before long, I was doing readings. I didn't charge anything for a long time. I hadn't even told my husband, children, mother, or sisters. Then one day while I was conducting a reading at our home with a young lady, my husband came home from work sick. I was busted. My husband just looked at us both and went to bed. He never said a word about it.

Stepping out of the Spiritual Closet

A few days went by and I couldn't take the fact I kept a secret from my husband. I asked if I could talk to him. He sat down and the words just spewed out of my mouth as I attempted to explain what I was doing and who I was. It was the first time I said, "I'm a medium." I asked him if he wanted a divorce and told him I understood if he did. I went on to explain I can't help who I am. He looked at me and told me he loved me no matter what. Even through all my hair color shades. I smiled, and I was relieved. I thought of Jim's statement years earlier. "You can't change your destiny." I finally accepted Jim was right.

The next task was to tell my mother, sisters, and children. Unfortunately, my mother and sisters were less than enthusiastic about my new title. My mother told me she and my sisters felt I was doing the devil's work. My two older children just listened and didn't say much when I told them. They were processing it. My youngest daughter, on the other hand, asked if her friends could come for readings.

I can honestly say I know the feeling of stepping out of the spiritual closet. I now have compassion for anyone stepping out of any closet and claiming their own truth. Even after finding the strength to claim who I am, I did not use my actual name at shows and expos. I still hid to some extent. I continued taking classes. I studied Numerology, Astrology, Human Design, Gene Keys, and Cards of Destiny. I can use eight different card systems for divination. And yet I was not confident in who I was or my abilities.

I often see spiritual healers, mediums, and psychics go through and experience horrific life lessons. I now know I could not be the medium I am today without going through extreme emotional pain. It helps me to feel and connect with the sitters. I have experienced the death of loved ones, loss of a child, emotional abuse, close family member murdered, family member the murderer, sexual abuse of my children, divorced twice, a child in prison, addictions, government agency injustices, and non-support of close family members and much, much more. I often thought after all I have been through it must have been my burning at the stake. Being confident and standing in my truth as a psychic medium should have been a piece of cake after all I went through. But for some reason, I still hid to some extent and only half-way acknowledged who I was.

Adam's Story

One spring day, I had a reading with a husband and wife from Des Moines, Iowa. They drove two and a half hours for their reading. The gentleman was a prominent surgeon and his wife a teacher. I always make it a practice to tell everyone that I only want their first name when they schedule a reading. That day I was expecting one person. I was a little surprised when two people showed up, but I have come to trust the spirit world knows best.

The first loved one in the afterlife I sensed connected to them was Adam. It was confirmed he was their only child. Adam was twenty-one years old when he passed away. He was attending college at the time. Adam was clear on the information he conveyed. His parents continued to validate every piece. Information and things do not always make logical sense to me, but eventually, the information makes perfect sense to the sitters. I have learned to trust the process.

In this reading, Adam showed me the entire house decorated for the holidays. He explained to me how his mom went over the top on her decorating, and he laughed. He showed me a dining room table with lots of pictures scattered as if someone had been going through the pictures. He even showed me a picture of the entire family that included the family dog. He kept telling his parents how sorry he was, and he didn't mean it. He said it was an accident.

As with many readings, Adam's mother cried the entire time. At the end of the hour, Adam's father explained to me their son struggled with addictions. He had been to treatment and was getting his life in order. He had come home from college for Christmas. They had hired a photographer to take family pictures on Christmas Eve afternoon. The photographer had emailed the pictures to them later in the evening, and he and his wife were going through the pictures on the dining room table. And yes, the dog was in every picture as well. We all laughed.

Christmas morning arrived. Adam's parents were making breakfast. When Adam didn't get up, his father went to wake him. Adam's father found his son in bed. He had passed away hours earlier from a drug overdose. Adam's passing happened two years earlier. Life had changed for their family in a blink of an eye. They had not celebrated a Christmas in two years. I felt their pain. I have children, and I don't even want to think about losing one of them, especially on a holiday such as Christmas. Adam's father went on to say the pictures lay on their dining room table for months after. That was the last interaction they had as a family. The three of them had been looking at the pictures before Adam retreated to bed. Readings like this break my heart.

The Gift of Mediumship

A month after my reading with Adam's parents, I received a telephone call from Adam's father. He wanted to thank me for everything I did for them. He told me I gave him his wife back. He went on to say, "What you did in one hour for my wife, a once a week appointment with a counselor for the past two years could not do for her. Your gift brings healing to families. I just wanted you to know how thankful I am." We chatted a bit, and he told me he was finally happy again, and his wife was going all out for the Christmas holidays again. I told him I was sure Adam would be pleased and present.

After I hung up the phone with Adam's father, I sat for a few minutes and reflected back over my life. All the mediumship courses I studied and the mentoring with well-known international mediums flashed in my mind. I sat in mediumship development circles with others wishing to develop their abilities weekly and spent countless hours developing and learning Numerology, Astrology, Human Design, Destiny of the Cards, and several other card systems. I read book after book and took workshops in order to further my development. I had attended numerous expos as a vendor and reader, given well over a thousand readings, lectured and even conducted many platform galleries professionally. But it wasn't until this one phone call I realized how my gift brought healing to others in such a profound way. It hit me like a ton of bricks. I no longer cared about the time or money I spent to learn and develop. My thoughts and heart were only focused on Adam and his parents. Due to my efforts and spiritual gifts I was able to reconnect Adam with his parents in order for healing to take place. Adam's parents had found the strength and courage to live again knowing they could reconnect with their son. I had helped to facilitate their love of life and each other after such a horrific tragedy.

That one phone call changed my entire perspective on conducting readings and standing in my truth. For years I had used the name In Love and Light in order to hide what I was doing from family, friends and the local community I lived in. I was so afraid of being exposed as a fraud and a bit crazy. I had still been hiding in the spiritual closet at the time of my reading with Adam's parents. After my phone call with Adam's father, I started using my actual name on all my business cards and literature. I no longer hid in the spiritual closet under another name. For the first time, I felt honored to have been given this gift to help bring loved ones together once more. I could see the healing that takes place in connecting loved ones in spirit with loved ones still living. That is the true gift of mediumship.

~

Chapter 3:

The Connection Process

*"Developing mediumship takes time
and effort. There are no short cuts.
There are no quick fixes. Developing
mediumship is a lifetime's work.
We never stop learning."*

—Martin Twycross

The Process

I have heard too many heartbreaking stories in the readings I do. I want to help bridge the two worlds together and educate people on how they can connect themselves. For that reason, I came up with a process so you can connect with your loved ones in the afterlife and see the signs they are leaving you. I call the process C.O.N.N.E.C.T.E.D. Over the next few chapters, I will walk you through each step and explain afterlife communication that is easy to understand and put into practice. Below is an outline of the steps.

C: Courage to See Beyond
You will examine how your emotions, beliefs, and thoughts are directly influencing your life.

At the end of this step, you will have a good understanding of how your childhood has impacted your views on life. You will learn how emotions and thoughts work together. By taking a closer look at your current beliefs and making small adjustments, you will clear the path for connecting to the afterlife.

O: One with Spirit

You will dispel Myth 1 about Prayer, Protection, and the White Light and have a clear understanding of why it is not necessary or important in connecting to your loved ones.

At the end of this step, you will feel comfortable and at ease in connecting to the Spirit World. You will be shown the difference between reality and what people have been taught. You will have a clear understanding of why there is nothing to fear.

N: No Judgment

You will dispel Myth 2. You will learn why you can combine both religion and spirituality and be at peace with both.

During this step, you will be introduced to different spiritual practices and the roles the different churches play. You will have a better understanding of suicide and purgatory and have a clear understanding of heaven and hell.

N: No Way. I Can Do This Like the Experts

You will dispel Myth 3. You will learn that mediums, psychics, and intuitives are not the only ones connected to the afterlife. We are all connected.

During this step, you will learn the difference between a medium, psychic, and intuitive. You will learn about spiritual gifts and soul evolution.

E: Education on Mediumship

You will learn the inconsistencies of mediumship and how to interpret the meaning of each.

At the end of this step, you will have a better understanding of some of the issues of mediumship and how to work around them. You will learn how to tell the difference between a guide providing you information and a loved one. There are many things in this chapter that will help you in the actual development of mediumship.

C: Commingling Energies

You will learn the importance of meditation and meditation techniques. You will also learn the importance of blending with Spirit.

During this step, you will learn the difference between blending with Spirit and meditation. You will learn the importance of each and the techniques and how to accomplish both. You will understand how implementing each in your daily rituals will help to connect with your loved ones in the afterlife.

T: The Language of Souls

In this step, you will learn the language of souls and how your loved ones communicate with you.

You will learn how your loved ones speak to you. You will learn how they use symbols and how the clairs are used in communication.

E: Experience Different Modalities

In this step, you will be introduced to a variety of modalities that can be used in communicating with your loved ones.

In this step, you will learn different divination systems that can be utilized in afterlife communication. You will gain an understanding of how synchronicity works in communicating with your loved ones. You will also learn when a visitation dream occurs.

D: Dang I'm Good

You will learn how to put all the previous steps together and test for results.

This step is a recap of everything you have learned. You will be given tips and techniques on how to put into practice the previous steps and to test the results for validation.

Dillon's Story

Three years ago, I attended a Paranormal Expo in Cedar Rapids, Iowa. At the expos and fairs I attend, I have a sign-up sheet on the table for clients to sign up for a specific time slot for a reading. I am usually fully booked and have no time to see who has signed up until I meet with them when they sit down for their reading.

Early in the morning, a young lady sat down. I asked her name, and she replied, "Jesse." She was beautiful. She was slender with long dark brown hair. I would estimate her age at late twenties. During the reading, she kept looking over her shoulder at a young gentleman who was leaning up against the wall at the end of the aisle. I knew there was some connection the two of them had from the way she looked at him. I sensed she was nervous. I also sensed her deep emotional pain. I asked, "Have you ever had a reading before?" Jesse replied, "No. This is the first time." I smiled and reassured her it would be okay.

During the reading, a young child appeared in my mind's eye. He was approximately three years old. I told Jesse this, and she confirmed she knew the child without telling me the connection. I went on to say he told me he is your son. Immediately, she burst into tears and turned to look at the young man against the wall. I then said to Jesse, "I am confused about what he is showing me, and I keep arguing with him that his information is not accurate, or perhaps I am not understanding it correctly. He insists he passed away while driving a car himself. He is even getting angry at me for not believing him. I tell him there is no way that is possible. But he keeps showing me his hands on the steering wheel and his foot on the gas." Jesse said, "He is correct." I looked at Jesse astonished and surprised. I said, "Don't tell me the story until the end of the reading. It will confuse the information I receive if I let my logical mind interfere." I looked at her son, and he laughed and said to me, "I told you so."

I said to Jesse, "I am getting a "D" connected to the name." She said, "Yes." This young child began showing me images of his father picking him up and looking at him. His father was searching for injuries but could find none. His body was limp. His father then carried him to his car and put him in the car. The child told me, "He is driving so fast." Then the car comes to a stop and an ambulance crew is taking him out of the car and moving him to the ambulance. He told me one of the people on the ambulance crew had tears as they worked on him.

In the end, there was nothing anyone could do to save him. He had already passed away almost immediately upon impact. He had no physical signs of trauma. It wasn't until receiving the autopsy results that an actual cause of death was known. The young child also told me to tell his mother she would have more children and then he laughed again and said to me, "Even if it is impossible now." Again, my logical mind was confused, and again I said to Jesse, "You can tell me at the end of the reading."

The young child was insistent. He told me to tell his mom he is leaving her signs, but she was ignoring him. Jesse looked at me in surprise. Then she turned to look at the young man again. She turned back and said to me, "We wondered but were not sure." Her son also told her to tell Dad hello. Again, Jesse looked at the young man. Her son also told them both to quit blaming themselves for what happened. He was adamant about the fact it was an accident.

At the end of the reading, Jesse explained to me what had happened. Her son's name was Dillon. He was three years old when he passed away. He was outside with his father in their backyard two months earlier. He was driving a vehicle that many children have. He drove it straight into a building. The impact thrust him into the steering wheel, and it severed an artery to his heart. That's why there were no physical signs of trauma. His father was in the backyard and witnessed the entire accident. He picked up Dillion, put him in the car and drove until he met up with the ambulance that had been dispatched to their home.

Dillon was their second-born child and their only son. Her husband had a vasectomy after he was born. After his passing, they had discussed having it reversed to have another child. I told her Dillion had said, "children." That indicated to me more than one. She was surprised. Jesse did say they had both blamed themselves for purchasing the toy vehicle and allowing him to drive it. I could tell she felt relief in what her son had said, "It was an accident."

Jesse told me she had seen the Paranormal Expo advertisement and forced her husband to come with her. He was the gentleman against the wall. Her husband told her he would go and support her, but he did not believe himself that afterlife communication was possible. She had signed up for the reading with me, and her husband told her he would wait by the wall until she had finished. She thanked me for the reading. She thought Dillion was leaving signs but the skeptical part of her dismissed the signs. She was glad I confirmed it. I gave Jesse a big hug and told her, "This is from Dillon."

I watched Jesse leave my booth, walk straight over to her husband. They exchanged a quick conversation between them and then walked back to my booth and headed straight to the sign-up sheet. Dillion's father booked a reading that would take place three hours later. That was the next available time slot. The reading later in the day between father and son was heartwarming and healing. There was so much love felt between the two of them even I cried. Even after all the readings I have conducted over the years, I am still in awe and wonderment when two hearts come together for love.

A few months after meeting with Dillion's parents, his mother Jesse phoned me. She wanted to set up another reading to learn how to recognize the signs from her son. She also informed me she just found out she was pregnant. She was happy. Over the next year, I spoke with Jesse several times, and we discussed how Dillon communicates with her and how she can recognize the signs. Today, Jesse is confident in interpreting the signs from Dillon. She no longer second-guesses the signs. Since Dillion's passing, Jesse has given birth to one child and is currently expecting another child. Dillion was right after all.

I have helped several individuals and families understand the signs their loved ones are sending them from the other side. In this book, I share the tips and techniques I have learned to help you see the signs as well. With the information provided here and a little bit of practice, you will gain the confidence needed to connect with your loved ones and test your results for validation.

Dillon started leaving signs for his parents immediately after his passing. He wanted them to know he was still there, and he loved them. He also wanted them to know it was an accident and to quit blaming themselves. Your loved ones have been leaving you signs as well. It is just a matter of learning the steps to connect. Are you ready? Your loved ones in spirit are.

$\sim$

Chapter 4:

Courage to See Beyond
Your Beliefs

*"What would life be if we had no
courage to attempt anything."*

—Vincent Van Gogh

The first step in the C.O.N.N.E.C.T.E.D. process is *Courage
to See Beyond*. In this chapter, you will examine how your
emotions, beliefs, and thoughts are directly influencing your life.
You will learn to recognize and understand how your childhood
has impacted your views on life. This is an important step in
your development. By closely examining many of your early
beliefs and making small adjustments, you will remove blocks
and then the doors to connect will open wide for you. All I ask
is that you keep an open mind. Being flexible with your mind
and beliefs will have a tremendous impact on your future ability
for connection.

Mind of His Own

It was approximately one month after my grandson was born
that I visited him for the second time. My son, his wife, and

newborn son live two and a half hours away from me. When I arrived in the evening, my son Cody and his wife Tiffany were getting my grandson ready for bed. My grandson was dressed in what appeared to me as a tight, body-snugging sleeping bag. His arms were inside the sleeping bag and it looked tight to his body. The only thing showing was his head. I asked what the bodysuit was, and it was explained to me it was a sleep sack and everyone is using them with their infant children. I asked, "How long does he wear it?" He wears it until he is one year old was the answer.

My mind raced. I looked at my son and his wife and said, "I don't know about you, but doesn't that seem a bit confining?" I never got a definite answer back other than, "That is what everyone is using. It reminds an infant of being in the womb." Hmm, I kept thinking. "Well, I am amazed that each of you survived just fine without a sleep sack when you were infants." Boy, did I get a lesson that day. No more bumper pads in cribs, no more sleeping on their stomachs. All infants are now laying on their backs when they are put to bed. Again, I looked at my son and said, "Eventually he will do what he wants, and that will be that." We all laughed.

A few months later when I visited again, my grandson was still in the sleep sack, but his arms were free to move about as he wished. I was informed he was being demanding about having his arms free. Suffice to say, he never made it a year in that sleep sack. He did have a mind of his own and was using it to communicate with his parents.

I tell you this story as an example of how often each of you follow what appears to be the latest and greatest trend or idea because others tell you to or the simple fact that others are doing it. I was just glad my son and his wife allowed their son to have some say in his sleeping comfort.

This is one of the first lessons you must learn in order to open the doors to the other side. You must have a solid foundation and the courage to look at yourself and your belief system just like my son and his wife. They followed what was taught at the time. After all, publicly, there was good medical information as to why the sleep sack worked. But as they also learned my grandson was determined to free his arms. Perhaps the protocol changes again and we go back to laying our infants on their stomachs again. No one knows what the future holds regarding infant care. But the point is this: They had no actual proof it worked, only what others were saying. They were listening to who they perceived as the experts in the field. And so, it became something they believed in until my grandson had his own ideas.

Childhood Beliefs

Every person alive is a product of their upbringing. Your beliefs were established long ago as a child. Your belief system more than likely is based upon your parents' and grandparents' beliefs. At times, a teacher may have had a significant influence on you as well. But for the most part, it was what was occurring in your home during your adolescent years that had the biggest impact.

Your core beliefs about money, work, relationships, college, et cetera will have a direct tie to your early development years. If you take the time and examine your life, you will discover your belief system is directly connected. Even your views on the afterlife were originally established during childhood. Movies you attended, friends, relatives, and your environment as a child all played a significant role. As you begin to mature, you continue playing the same belief record over and over. You keep going through the same motions that you have always done because of what you have always believed. You tend to react the same way to situations over and over. If you were brought up in a Christian home, guess what? Your beliefs will likely align with other Christians. The same if you were brought up in a welfare home. Your belief system becomes that of the welfare system. Childhood patterns were established long ago, and these patterns directly affect your current belief system.

You can change your childhood beliefs that keep repeating in adulthood. It takes time and effort to closely examine all your childhood beliefs. When you start to put it all together in connecting to the other side, you will see the relevance of this step and how it is extremely important to be open to all possibilities. Are your beliefs about certain things rooted in your upbringing? Is your belief what you were taught or based upon your actual experience?

Take the next few days and make a mental note as to where you developed your opinions and beliefs about any and everything. It can be on what diet is best, what vehicle is best, what political candidate you align yourself to, what color of clothing you feel looks best on you, et cetera. These internal opinions are happening several times throughout your entire day. Most of the time, you pay no attention at all to how you determine your choices. It just becomes decisions that happen as if your autopilot is on.

It is time for you to look at your belief system and how it was established in your life. Did you come to the belief through your experience, or did someone else lay the groundwork for that belief to exist? Take some time and think about all the different beliefs you have regarding anything and everything.

Consciousness Identity

In order for you to understand how and why you think the way you do, you must also examine how you identify with a specific consciousness. We are all connected through our consciousness. The physical body is just the clothing you wear in this life. Your consciousness is your thoughts. Your thoughts are the keys to your existence, and your emotions are the fuel to make it run. Often people will say someone is driving them crazy. The only way that can truly happen is if they asked someone else to chauffeur them around. You and only you have the keys. Are you driving, or is someone else? In other words, are you a self-thinker, or do you just go with what others are thinking and saying?

There are many forms and planes of consciousness occurring simultaneously each day. Look at the political consciousness taking place. Most people will tell you they identify with one party or the other. However, if you press them, most people have no idea why. Perhaps their parents or grandparents identified with that party. Perhaps their friends identify with that political party. If you were to ask someone to tell you ten things their party of choice stands for, most people are clueless. They are like sheep just following the herd. What happens is that they have gotten caught up in a specific form or group consciousness. And once you are caught in it, you have a hard time breaking away. It's like being dragged through a washing machine and you keep going around and around. Just watch the news, and you will quickly see this exact concept at work. Most news programs today identify with one specific consciousness. Don't you find it hard to believe that everyone who works at the same news station thinks alike? Even my husband and I don't always think alike. There is much truth to the old saying "birds of a feather flock together." It has to do with the consciousness everyone shares.

What consciousness have you identified yourself with? Examples to ponder are Facebook posts you like. Do you enjoy seeing public figures suffer? Is it better to have a college education or not? Can you only get rich by working hard?

States of Consciousness

There are different levels or states of consciousness each soul resides within as it progresses and evolves. The lowest state is for the new souls. The next state is the souls that are in the herd state. They follow the crowd. Then there is the individual state. It is where the soul begins to break away from the herd state and to decide for themselves without the input of others. The final state is the spiritual state. In this state, you will begin to see things from a highly evolved spiritual state, and you will have a good understanding of the school of life itself. Both ends of the spectrum from young to old souls do exist and each of you falls within a level. You have had specific times throughout your life that you can see how this works. I remember a time when I identified with drugs and alcohol. I followed the crowd. I'm sure you can imagine where this falls on the scale. I was stuck there for a few years and found comfort in others who were in the same state. It was a way of life. Eventually, I did break away but not without experiencing this level to its fullest.

Look at your life through a microscope. Where do you see yourself in identifying with the different states of consciousness? Where are you putting and giving your energy to? Honestly, most people don't even think about it. But if you want to expand and grow your level of awareness, you must look deep into your existence. If you can, you will begin to shift in your awareness to know thyself, and that is where the magic happens in connecting to the other side.

Soul Patterns

The soul knew long before it entered the physical body exactly what it came to learn. It is aware of the mode in which it will learn the exact lessons laid out on the journey. If you are reading this, then you are ready to move beyond the lower levels of consciousness and have opened the door to step outside the sheep mentality which exists in at least seventy percent of the population today. A small percentage of the population has moved beyond into the higher states of consciousness. You will see this play out in how you interact with each other, how you treat one another.

There is a soul age, but I don't want you to get hung up on it and begin to judge others or yourself. It has nothing to do with age, but more to do with the lessons you have learned over your entire soul's existence. This is the one dimension where all levels of souls from old to young exist. It is the school of life, and we are all here to learn and to grow. Each person wants to grow and gain knowledge in order to evolve into a higher version of self.

When you complete this life, you will have achieved, completed, and mastered many things your soul desired.

Understanding your soul patterns gives you the ability to see how it is you learn things. You may learn through your thoughts, which is learning mentally. You may learn through your emotions. Your emotions will push you to move forward as you experience emotions that are uncomfortable. You will find yourself desiring to move past what you are feeling. And some souls will even learn through the day to day physical experiences. There is no right or wrong way; it is just what your soul chose. When you get back home to the other side, you can ask all the questions as to why you chose what you did. I know it is one of the first questions I am asking.

The main lesson to remember is, in the end, your entire life will come down to memories of feelings. You will remember your emotional reaction to events throughout your life. It is not what you did but how you felt about it. This is what pushes you forward and the true magic of evolution.

Owning My Truth

I had a close childhood friend named John. He would always talk to me about his chosen spiritual lifestyle. He wanted so badly to be himself, but he was scared to death what his parents and community would think of him. For years, he hid in a self-imposed closet, unable to stand in his truth. I felt sorry for him and thought it was such a shame for him to live in fear of being exposed and judged. I was so happy for him when he called to tell me he came clean. He was out of the closet to his parents. It was like a new light was shining in him. I could feel his sense of calm and peace. He was finally able to be free and to be who he wanted to be.

You as well must be willing to step out of the spiritual closet. It was the most difficult thing I have ever done. I have so much compassion and can relate to my friend John and others in his situation. Standing in your truth can feel like having a spotlight shining on you, and your life is opened to scrutiny. Others will judge you. That is a fact. But honestly, others are probably already judging you in other areas of your life. I figure I was probably burned at the stake in a previous life; what's one more? My loved ones and spirit friends on the other side deserve more respect and love than me feeling ashamed of what I am and what I do. I owe it to them, and I owe it to myself to be myself. I now stand in my truth and can honestly say I love who I am and what I do.

It doesn't mean you need to go out with a bullhorn and announce it on the street corner. But it does mean to feel proud of what you are doing. To be yourself and to stand in your truth. Your soul knows exactly what it is doing. You are not here to hide. You are here to be proud of who you are, to shine your inner light. You are also setting the example for many others who are still in the spiritual closet. You are here to help raise each other one step at a time, one soul at a time.

Life Purpose

As a psychic, I get asked the question about life purpose over and over. I think most people get confused between life purpose and career. It is true some souls will choose a life of bringing healing to others, and some souls will choose a life of teaching others. And yet there are souls who will just hold the light and space for others to do their thing in life so they can experience every aspect of the human existence. In the end, we all have the same life purpose. We all want to evolve, to grow, and to learn, to expand our consciousness.

If you want to evolve quickly, then you must be of service to others. Being of service to others is the highest form of love you can demonstrate to another, and love is what it is all about. You are a spark of the divine. You are love in action. Even though you look around at the world and all that is happening, you begin to wonder why. How can this be a demonstration of love? But it is. Loving unconditionally with no judgment of other's actions is the epitome of evolution. Acceptance of others and sending loving thoughts and emotions their way has more impact than you probably realize.

Often, I find myself struggling with having no judgment of others. I still judge my children's decisions on life. I remember when my daughter wanted to be a funeral director. I was worried about her in such a depressing career. I also wondered what level of success she could obtain in a field that has been typically dominated by men. I didn't like the hours and holidays that her career would demand. I thought about how difficult it would be for her to have a family. In the end, she was right about her decision. I can't count the number of times someone has stopped me and told me how much they appreciated all my daughter did for their family in their time of grief. Even though I had a judgment about her career choice, I came to the conclusion she needed to live her own life. I just need to love her unconditionally and to help, be of service, when it is needed. I am a work in progress. I know I am not done evolving.

Reality and Imagination

Reality and imagination are so close your ideas and thoughts can get confused and mix things up. You get hung up on what your perception of reality is when the actual reality is this world is in your imagination. You are experiencing it and looking at it from your higher self or your higher level of consciousness. The body your soul inhabits is not real. It will die and decay. The animals and the plants are not real either. They will also die and decay. The entire planet and dimension are created by all of us to learn from experiences. It is a hard concept to accept. The entire system is set up for your evolution, your school of higher soul education, and nothing that happens goes without some benefit to that process. Many people ask, "Why would we go through all this hell?" We all learn differently, and some of us need lessons to slap us in the face, so we make necessary adjustments to our lives. When you pass away and return home, you will look back and see during your life review that you learned a lot. You have evolved, and every hardship was a valuable lesson in disguise. The one thing I have learned is the more you evolve and ascend, the less you know. It is the process of aligning with the actual concept that life is an illusion and not real after all.

To illustrate this further, think of how you create your thoughts moment by moment. You are constantly changing your thoughts at your whim. Perhaps you have a thought to save the whales. That thought is directly connected to your soul's higher self. It is a thought based on service and love. Once you have that thought, you may choose to act upon it by forming an organization with other like-minded people. The organization may petition lawmakers to change the laws regarding whales. All of this originated in your thoughts. In your thoughts, you imagined and dreamed about saving the whales, and then, in reality, you can see the outcome.

The earth we live on is constantly changing. The save the whales story is just one of the many thoughts and ideas in your imagination that plays out. You and everyone else are creating the world you live in. In fact, our laws became a reality because someone had the original thought in their imagination. Creation is a byproduct of what you dream and imagine. Fascinating, don't you think?

Thoughts and Emotions

Your thoughts and emotions work hand-in-hand. Just think how boring life would be if there were no emotions whatsoever – love being the highest emotion of all, and fear, hate and anger being as low as your emotions can go. Your thoughts are similar to the car you drive, and your emotions are the fuel that propels it. Your thoughts often judge a person, place or thing. He is fat, she has too many tattoos, I'm ugly, the teacher cannot teach, she is pretty, he is hot. These are all thoughts you have daily. All day, every day, thoughts are going through your mind. Some thoughts have no emotion attached at all. Other thoughts can produce intense emotions. For example, if I looked at the grass and think, winter must be coming. It is turning brown. I honestly have no emotion attached to it. It is a stated fact. If I see my husband talking to a pretty young girl and I think she is pretty and young, then I may attach the emotion of jealously to it or anger at my husband for even speaking to her. Or perhaps on a higher level of emotion, I may feel blessed that he chose me with all my flaws and not the pretty young girl he is talking to.

Since we communicate with the other side through our consciousness, your loved ones are understanding every thought and emotion you are experiencing. The more positive your emotions, the higher and more refined the vibrational energy you are demonstrating. You are constantly in a state of vibration. The longer you can stay in the higher states of love, compassion, service, empathy, kindness, joy, happiness, et cetera, the easier it will be for you to connect with your loved ones who have passed. Sorrow, anger, hate, and jealousy will make your vibrational energy slow and sluggish. These are low-level emotions. They slow your progress. They keep you stuck, unable to move forward.

Every day, your thoughts and emotions are constantly matching a similar vibration. If you have emotional thoughts of sadness, then the universe works to match and deliver to you a matching vibration. Often you hear this referred to as the law of attraction. You will attract into your life exactly how you feel. Sadness can cause you to feel tired. Because of this, you will experience a slower vibration. Your loved ones are in a place of love, compassion, joy, et cetera. Therefore, they are upbeat, and this makes their vibration quicker. If you are at a lower-level vibration and they are at a higher vibration, then there can be a mismatch of energies. That will make it difficult to connect easily. Remember, you can always change your emotional state. It just involves changing your thoughts.

When you connect with the other side, you are working to increase your vibrational energy. It is like tuning a radio dial to an exact station. The higher your vibration, the purer your thoughts and emotions are and the clearer the channel. The trick is to maintain it for a length of time. There are some tips, tricks, and exercises we will talk about in future chapters in order to help you. Remember, you will automatically get a high vibrational boost because you want to connect with your loved ones out of love, the highest vibration possible. Your vibratory rate is determined by your thoughts, emotions, attitudes, and spiritual understanding.

As your views and thoughts become established, you will feel most comfortable around others that have many of the same opinions and beliefs. If you physically attend a bar every night for happy hour, you will find you can relate and have an energetic connection to others doing the same thing. Your energies are a close match. You feel most comfortable with them. That is the vibration you are emitting while at the bar. This occurs daily. It is important to take a look at your life and answer a few questions.

What level of vibration are your thoughts and emotions? Do you see the glass as half empty or half full? Can you quickly change your thoughts and emotions at whim? Do you hang on to low-level emotions? Can you find happiness in life throughout the major part of your day?

Courage to Look at Self

Looking at your life using a realistic approach and diving deep into your beliefs and thought process will give you an indication as to where you are in the evolutionary process. If you can be honest when you do this, you can break away from the lower-level consciousness state and move to the higher levels. This is an important step for you to connect with your loved ones in spirit. It is not an exercise to beat up on yourself for your beliefs and thoughts, but it has more to do with acknowledging and identifying where you need to shift your thoughts. It is a process that never ends throughout your life.

All Is Not as It Appears

From a young age, I have heard the statement "All is not as it appears" over-and-over again from the spirit world. I often would ask, "What does that mean?" And honestly, it annoyed me. It was always at the strangest times in my life, and I never could quite connect the dots. A couple of years ago, my family experienced a horrific tragedy. Finally, after more than five decades, I finally understood that saying. It became crystal clear to me, as I stated earlier. The higher you evolve, the less you actually know.

My advice to you is to be flexible with your thoughts and beliefs. Do not back yourself into a corner on anything. What you think and have a judgment about is more than likely the farthest thing from the truth. We are seeing some of it play out on a large scale. People and things are being exposed at an alarming rate and will continue to be exposed for several years to come. Your role is to become the observer. Do not take sides or pass judgment because as soon as you do, your world will be turned upside down, and you will find yourself caught back up in the washing machine. Remember, it is all about evolution, not revolution.

~

Chapter 5:

You Are Always Protected

*"We are one heart, one
love, and one spirit."*

—Panache Desai

Last year, I attended a holistic expo in Minneapolis, Minnesota. At that expo, I was a guest lecturer. The lecture itself was titled Channeling 101 which has always been a popular lecture. At the end of my lectures, I always open it up to questions from the audience. A gentleman asked me to go over my protocol before I do readings or connect with the other side. I quizzed him further as to what he meant. He asked if I protect myself from negative energy and if I put a white light around myself? This question prompted me to ask the entire audience to raise their hands if they believed they needed to protect themselves, if they used sage, and if they surrounded themselves with white light. There were approximately 150 in attendance. I was surprised and astonished to see every single person in the audience raise their hand. I told the audience it was important I help educate them on my understanding from my experience. I want to share the same information with you as well.

The second step in the C.O.N.N.E.C.T.E.D. process is One with Spirit. In this step, you will dispel the first myth about prayer, protection, and the white light. By the end of this chapter, you will understand why it is not necessary for connecting to the other side. You will feel a sense of peace in connecting to the spirit world and a clear understanding that there is nothing to fear.

Childhood Visitors and Protection

It was not uncommon for me to have nighttime visitors as a child. Like I said earlier, in the beginning, they scared the crap out of me because I didn't know what they wanted from me. I was unable to communicate with them, so I hid under my covers and kept asking them to go away. I have heard and read about young children having similar experiences. Adults have attached the name of imaginary friends. As time went on, these visitors did become my friends, my support system. They were dependable, and I could always talk to them. I need to clarify the term talking. It is not speaking like you and I do. It would be described as a conversation going on in my head. It is a thought process.

No one ever told me to be afraid or to protect myself. I never learned anything about the white light, how to use sage, or protection until more than twenty years later. And yet, my spirit companions had been there all those years. It had never crossed my mind to be afraid of them once I learned to connect and to communicate with them. In fact, they have been helping me, teaching me, and comforting me my entire life.

Honestly, people in the physical world, on the other hand, scare the hell out of me. They murder each other, rape each other, steal from each other, and lie to each other. They will take care of themselves first and even sell their first child if it serves their ego. They lock their cars, lock their houses, and don't completely trust their own family, friends or neighbors. They post negative comments on the internet and say the most hurtful things to each other.

Every day, you go out into the world with no thought of protecting yourself from all the negativity going on around you. You navigate your everyday life through a minefield of negative energy daily. And you're worried about the spirit side? In all honesty, and if I look at the facts, I trust the other side, my spirit friends, before I would trust most of the population. If I were to take a poll, and I have, you all don't trust each other either. I can pick up the newspaper in any major city, look at the news on the internet or TV and read or hear about crimes humanity is constantly committing against each other. And yet, if I took another poll, and I have, no one has ever listened to, read or seen an article or news story about a spirit committing the same daily atrocities at the same level or numbers. Hmm, I think I will take my chances with the other side. Most people I interact with appear to be the crazy ones.

I have no idea where this idea or belief of protection and surrounding yourself with the white light ever got started. Even high level, spiritual mentors and teachers are teaching this to people who are beginning on their spiritual path. So rather than teaching about love, they are breeding more fear. Seems backward to me since fear is a lower-level emotion and thought vibration. The lower the thought vibration, the more difficult it is to connect with the other side. It makes it that much harder for evolution to naturally occur and for people to break out of the fear-based consciousness so they can connect with their loved ones.

I often think about the Hopi Indians. You can learn much from them. The Hopi acknowledge that witchcraft exists. They have a good understanding of the levels and states of consciousness and that each soul is learning and evolving at its own rate. They also understand that each of us has free will and can at any time participate in a specific level of consciousness. They also believe in living from the heart and the best defense is to live with a pure, humble heart. When you do that, negativity cannot affect you. If you allow others to affect you, then you are giving credence to the lower vibrations and increasing the size of the lower-level consciousness. Live with humility and love despite anything going on around you. The Hopi belief is one of a much higher vibration. I'm disappointed in many of our current spiritual teachers. They should be teaching about love, compassion, and acceptance like the Hopi and stay away from fear.

Having trust and faith is the best protection there is. Your loved ones on the other side do not want you to be afraid of them. They want you to be at peace with their passing and their new mode of life. When you think about it, why would they scare you? Believe me; it is not their intention. Now having a little fun with you from time to time is something they will do. I tease my kids all the time that when I die and transition to the other side, I'm going to stalk them. I'm going to invade their dreams, move items around in their house just so they know I am still there. I think it's going to bc fun.

Prayer

I learned about prayer in my Christian studies as a child. I can't tell you the number of times I have recited the Lord's Prayer.

I have gone through the motions over and over, never even paying attention to what I was saying. I'm sure many of you can relate to the same thing. I have come to believe that in order for prayer to work, it must come from the heart. It is a time to be honest with yourself. Prayer is not just a time to beg for things when you are in a desperate situation. I do ask for guidance and assistance from my spirit friends. But the most common prayer I recite consists of thank you. Thank you for coming through and helping me in a reading, and thank you for supporting me during a reading. I always tell the other side I couldn't do it without them. The gratitude I feel for the other side is beyond words.

There have also been times in my life that I have been in situations and life experiences that have brought me to my knees asking for help and guidance from the other side. I have come to a place of surrender and humility when praying for help. During times of suffering, the largest growth and evolution is taking place, for with each heartache comes growth of the soul. The tears you shed are the water needed for the new seeds to grow. You are essentially watering your garden.

I do not feel I need to pray at certain or specific times for protection. If anything, I pray to be protected from humanity. My friends in spirit know my heart and know my thoughts and emotions. They know your heart as well. They know what you seek before you ever utter a word in prayer.

Prayer should be a conversation with Source, God, the Divine. Whatever context works for you and you feel comfortable with. It can also be a conversation with your loved ones in the afterlife or your spirit guides. Think of it as if you are having a cup of coffee with a good friend pouring your heart out to them. I feel fortunate to have a couple of super close friends that allow me to do that. Our conversations consist of my life concerns, my hopes and dreams, and my joys and celebrations. That is the purpose of prayer. Loved ones and your guides on the other side are always listening to every thought you have, especially if you are thinking of them.

Sage and Clearing Energy

Using sage to clear a space is common among metaphysical practitioners. You can hire someone to come to your property, or you can purchase sage and do the clearing yourself. I admit I participated in this practice myself for a few years. I had no idea why I was doing it other than a spiritual teacher taught how it is done. I even went as far as to learn an egg cleansing technique known as Limpia. It is popular in Mexico and Ecuador. It is used as a spiritual cleansing to remove moods, emotions, and energy imprints that no longer are in your best interest. I must admit I was fascinated by the egg results.

Since I participate in paranormal investigations from time to time, occasionally a client will hire me to tour their home as they feel they are experiencing paranormal activity. A few years ago, I had one such client named Amy. Amy had been experiencing a kitchen cabinet door opening and closing. She often would wake in the morning and find the door wide open. I spoke to her over the phone and instructed her to do the opposite just to see if someone from the other side was playing tricks on her. So, one night she did the opposite and left the cabinet door wide open. And sure enough, just as I had expected, it was closed the next morning.

Now you can imagine how excited Amy was. Honestly, Amy was hysterical. She inquired as to how soon I could get to her house and clear out all the negative energy. I scheduled a visit the next day. Upon entering her home, I felt nothing but love from the other side. I sensed her grandmother right away. I even picked up the previous homeowner that provided me with specific information about the house. A few days after my visit, Amy made a trip to the local courthouse and researched the information provided. Amy was able to confirm the previous homeowner's information and that it was accurate.

During my tour of Amy's home, she confirmed the kitchen was the only area in the home where the activity occurred. She also confirmed it was the same kitchen cabinet door every time. So, I asked her deceased grandmother to help with what was occurring. Her grandmother instructed me to look directly above the cabinet. The kitchen cabinets in Amy's home had an open soffit and did not go all the way to the ceiling. I stood on a chair and reached above. Amy and I were shocked at what I found. I grabbed a small bag of marijuana from above the cabinet. Amy later learned it belonged to her sixteen-year-old son. Here, all along, her grandmother was trying to tell her to look above the cabinet. This is a prime example of what many times is help from your loved ones. Her grandmother was just trying to get her attention, but Amy could not think beyond the opening and closing of the cabinet door and her fears of the other side encouraged her thoughts to run wild.

The last piece of advice I have on this topic is the following. If someone insists your property or space is being haunted by negative energy, ask them to be specific and provide details on who it is or what it is. If they are gifted enough to pick up that kind of energy information, then they should be able to tell you exactly what or who it is. Often, the energy they pick up is what is going on in your thoughts and emotions or another family member's thoughts and emotions that are directly connected to the house or location. It may be a leftover energy imprint left from an occurrence that took place earlier.

What many people don't realize is that by using sage and clearing property, you are clearing out everything. All energy is moved and cleared out. Even your loved ones, such as Amy's grandmother, would have been removed. That is why I am no longer so quick to react. I want to know more about the energy and what is going on. There are times to sage and times to not sage.

Pipe Tobacco

My husband and I purchased a piece of property that included eleven acres of land. There is a large building located on the property that was once known as a county home. Most people would call it a nursing home. The property is located three miles outside the nearest town in the country. At the time we purchased the property, the building had ninety-eight percent of all windows broken out of it, and from the looks of the inside, it had been used as a drug haven. It had been abandoned for approximately seven years. When I first stepped onto the property, it felt dead to me. The land itself felt just like the building I was looking at. All the animals had even abandoned the property. I knew from what my spirit friends were saying that it would be alright, that my husband and I could return the property to a place of peace and serenity, and when we did, all the animals would return. What they didn't tell me was how that would occur.

A short time after the purchase of the property, we started renovations to turn the property into apartments. This was a big project, and we had anticipated it would take three years to complete. Approximately one year after we started, I had a phone reading with a woman from Michigan who was wanting to connect with her mother in the afterlife. It was the first time I had ever spoken to her. She did not tell me until the end of the reading that she was also a medium, and she had Native American roots. Her direct ancestors were Native American. She conveyed to me her deceased ancestors knew of the land my husband and I had purchased. She told me they were asking me to slowly walk and drop pipe tobacco around the perimeter of the entire land and, while I was doing it, to recite a blessing asking the Great Spirit to bless the land and to make it whole again so the animal kingdom would return and it would become a place of peace.

Hours later, I did just what was asked of me. The next day, three deer were on our property, and a raven flew overhead then landed and perched in a tree staring at me as I was walking the dogs. I knew the land had been blessed. A deer is a sacred symbol. It is a symbol of spiritual authority. The number three is a sacred number as well. It is the number of the trinity, and the raven is a symbol of overcoming difficulties. A raven's message is that all things will work out. Two days later while taking a walk on the property, I found a raven feather. It sits on a shelf in my reading room today as a reminder of what I learned from the pipe tobacco experience.

I no longer use sage to clear energy as to clear would be a negative, lower vibration. I now bless the property and the land, asking for it to be returned to a place of peace and serenity just like Amy's deceased grandmother who was present in Amy's house. When blessing the property, any soul from spirit can remain if they are demonstrating love, and any other energies that are not in alignment with the blessing will be removed automatically by my request of the other side. Your loved ones and guides can make suggestions, but it is still your free will, thoughts, and emotions that are in control of what takes place. I don't want to clear out my father, grandparents, or any other loved ones. I want to feel and sense them around. That is what gives me peace and serenity, and to bless is a high vibration, thus being positive and not negative. It makes more sense to me after what I have learned.

As Above, so Below

This is another saying I have heard from spirit several times. At various times throughout my life, I have quietly sat and written on paper the thoughts those in the spirit world were conveying to me. The best way to describe this is similar to the task of taking dictation. I have notebook upon notebook of journaling over the span of more than twenty years that the saying "As Above, so Below" has been recorded in channeled writings. The statement is made regarding our consciousness above in spirit is also our consciousness below in the physical world. Each soul does have an age that is also tied to their education level on what lessons they have learned spiritually. When you pass away, you do not suddenly become enlightened as many people think. In the spirit world, you don't have an ego, but your soul's level of experience and education remains the same. Evolution occurs as a process of development. If you look around in your surroundings and pay attention, you will notice the difference between an old soul and a young soul. Older and mature souls have a "we" mentality. They want to help others and know we are all in this together. The teenage and younger souls live in a world that demonstrates a "me" mentality. They are more concerned with the idea of "what's in it for me?"

All ages of souls live in unity on earth, and all levels of souls live in the spirit world as well. The younger souls often behave in ways that are a low vibration due to their thoughts and emotions. They often demonstrate a selfish attitude and only want what is best for themselves. That does not make one level or soul age superior to another. It just means one has hit the books more to learn and is, therefore, more expanded in its knowledge. The problem comes in when people associate negative energy with youthfulness of the soul. Think of how a two-year-old behaves. We as responsible adults do not find fault in a two-year-old's immaturity. We correct their behavior when it is unacceptable and wrong, and we chalk it up to their age. As adults, we should also be setting the example of how mature people should behave and act whenever we interact with children. The actual age of a person living does not tie to the soul age. You can encounter a ten-year-old that acts more responsible than an eighty-year-old. That is a direct reflection of the soul age.

Many times, our perception of someone is that they are evil because of their behavior. Once you understand this concept, you will begin to shift how you see other people and hopefully begin to see them through the eyes of love and understanding, knowing they are doing the best they can based on their evolution level. Our spirit friends do not judge anything we do. They understand the evolution process extremely well.

I also have heard people say the devil made them do it when referring to other people's actions and behavior. The truth of the matter is everyone has free will. In the end, the action people demonstrate is based on their own choices, barring a medical condition. Even Eve chose to eat the apple. No one forced it down her throat.

You need an ego in order to exist on earth. I often hear spiritual teachers tell their students to remove the ego as if they are saying there is a problem with the ego. Try going to the doctor and asking for your ego to be cut out because it is causing you problems. Your doctor would have no way of knowing how or where to look for your ego. And if the ego was entirely removed, it would change who you are. The ego is important. It gives you willpower and drive. It helps with confidence and is your internal survival instrument, which is only needed in the physical body and not in the afterlife. The key is to evolve to a point where the ego and soul are in alignment together, both working toward the same goals. At some point, they do ride in the same car together, and one does not try to override the other. They become teammates. Until a certain level of growth occurs, most people will demonstrate a lopsidedness that is an indication that the ego is more in charge, which is often perceived as negative energy.

There are all levels of souls on both sides of the veil. Just because someone is demonstrating selfishness does not make them negative. Evolutionary astrology points out that approximately seventy percent of our world population will behave selfishly as they are in the early stages of their development as a young soul. And only five percent of the world population has evolved to an old soul status. Until you have no judgment about anyone or anything and can see the illusion for what it is, you have not attained the top five percent. Based on just that, I have a lot to learn. As I already mentioned, my evolution and spiritual studies will continue as I do have judgment regarding people, places, and things.

Over the next few days, become a people watcher. Study their behavior and their motives. Are they living a life based on "me," or are they living their life based on "we?" Pay attention to your actions as well. On which end of the spectrum are you living your life?

~

Chapter 6:

Religion and Spirituality

*"People take different roads seeking
fulfillment and happiness.
Just because they're not on your road
doesn't mean they've gotten lost."*

—Dalai Lama

The third step in the C.O.N.N.E.C.T.E.D process is No
Judgment. In this step, you will dispel myth two. You will
learn how you can combine both religion and spirituality and be
at peace with both. During this step, you will be introduced to
different spiritual practices and the roles the different churches
play. At the end of this step, you will have a better understanding
of suicide, purgatory, heaven, and hell.

I recently conducted a reading with a young woman by the
name of Cindy. Cindy shared with me at the start of the reading
that she was extremely nervous and skeptical. She had been
studying to become an ordained minister in her Christian faith.
She had spoken to her current minister, and he had frowned
on her coming to see me. She explained to me how scared
she was. Her minister, friends, and family had all warned her
against getting a reading as they believed it was evil. I knew
the only reason she came was the power of love. The love she

felt for a certain family member was beyond what any minister, family, or friends could understand. Six months prior to her visit with me, she had lost her twin sister to cancer. Her sister was forty-three years old. They had been best friends and did everything together. Her love was so strong she was willing to risk everything she had been taught or believed in just to speak to her sister one more time.

Tears streamed down Cindy's face the entire reading. I could feel her sister's love from the other side. It was a bond the two of them had carried a lifetime, a special bond that only twin siblings can understand. When the reading was over, Cindy was grateful and asked how soon she could return. She had gone against her religious beliefs and other's warnings. She no longer cared about others' opinions. She did all this for the love of her sister, and she was glad she did.

Cindy's story is not unique in my line of work. I have heard similar stories so many times that it is heartbreaking. It gives me a sense of hope for humanity when people follow their hearts and step out of what I refer to as the spiritual closet. Love is the most powerful and highest vibrational emotion of all, and it can move us to do heroic things. It pushes us to see beyond our limiting beliefs. It gives us courage. If only we could stay in the vibration of love for eternity in the physical world.

All Souls Go Home

Whether you live in China, Japan, Sweden, or America, all souls will go to the same place when their physical body dies. Older, well-developed mediums call it Summerland. I often refer to it as the Home of the Souls. Your race, ancestry, and gender are all part of the physical body which only applies to your physical existence. There is no distinction on the other side. Just souls interacting with each other on an energetic vibration.

As I stated in the previous chapter, there is much truth to the saying "birds of a feather flock together" on both sides of the veil. You will always hang out with others that are at your current level of evolution. They help you, and you help them to evolve and develop. Your soul age is based on your level of evolution. Your personality remains the same when you pass away. You will still have your personality, thoughts, and memories. You can display emotions as well as you do in the physical dimension, but in my experience, all lower emotions such as hate, anger, et cetera, are not demonstrated by those in spirit during any readings I have conducted. The lower-level emotions are often associated with the ego, and the ego does not remain with you in the afterlife.

Various Religions

A few years ago, there were over 300 religious organizations who were organized and practicing religions. As a child, my family identified with the Lutherans and their beliefs. I'm sure you can imagine how difficult it was for me sitting in some of the church classes. I always had a spirit friend who was quite adamant with an opinion on specific teachings. I often would think, "Here we go again."

The most important lesson I learned and took away from my spirit friend was the variety of beliefs that were associated with every organization. Since I was raised as a Christian, I followed

Christ's teachings. If I had been raised in the Buddhist faith, I would have followed Buddha's teachings, and if I was raised as a Native American, I would have followed the teachings of the Great Spirit. I often imagined growing up in the Amazon jungle wondering what belief they followed. You could visit several places in the world and see several different spiritual practices being practiced today.

It doesn't matter what belief or organization you follow; in the end, all roads lead home. One form is no better or worse than another unless it is a radical group following lower emotional thoughts demonstrating hate, revenge, murder, et cetera. Just because I was raised Lutheran does not make my religious beliefs any better than another. If I was to think mine was better, then I would be judging others. The true teaching of any religion is do they walk the talk? Are they living a life of love and service? In the end, that is all that matters.

Each religion has its own set of issues and problems. If man could leave his opinions out of it, religions would have many more members and be much more successful. The savvy new age spiritual person sees this and is turned off by the strict rules. The decline in church membership over the past several years confirms this. It is disheartening to see this occurring. There has also been a steady increase in inhumane things that have occurred under the disguise of the church. These atrocities have been and are currently being exposed.

As with Cindy's church beliefs, many religious leaders are against the new age spiritual teachings and practices. What I learned as a child in church often inspired me. I knew if religion was used for good, we could move mountains. It was always a struggle for me hiding who I was, and it was difficult sitting through a church service listening to two sermons – one in person and one from my spirit friend finding it necessary to make corrections. After my children were confirmed, I stepped away from church for a few years until everything came full circle when circumstances in life became unbearable for my immediate family. I returned to church but not without changing to the Presbyterian church. My husband and I looked for a church family and pastor we enjoyed. It was never about having a belief; I could never change churches.

Looking back, I can see that I left the church based upon a belief I developed that I had heard from other spiritual teachers, mentors, and friends. One day while I was questioning what my spiritual mentors were teaching and my own newfound spiritual beliefs that were different from theirs, I asked my spirit friends to give me some sort of sign I could hold on to as I was struggling with a direction and what was real. I had reached a crossroads in my life, and I was confused. I had grown up in the church system and their beliefs. I had studied under well-known spiritual mentors and their beliefs, and yet I was still interacting with my spirit friends who often had an entirely different take on life than either the church or my spiritual mentors. It often seems that people in the metaphysical world dislike organized religions immensely. And the organized religion's belief is that mediums are evil. I often wondered where did that leave me? Was I a freak? As I sat with the Bible, I took a deep breath and asked my friends in spirit to show me something I could understand and believe in. I opened the Bible to 1 Corinthians 14:1 which says, "Follow the way of love and eagerly desire gifts of the Spirit, especially prophecy." I no longer question anything. And as years earlier, I am listening again to two sermons. I can see a lot of good that

71

comes in my attending church. Even in my little country church of forty-four members, from time to time, someone will approach me at a Sunday morning service and whisper in my ear, "I loved your last Facebook post." They were referring to my Kim Weaver Evidential Medium and Channel page. It makes me giggle inside knowing I'm making an impact even on church members. At last, I'm at peace that it is okay to straddle both beliefs, and I feel there are many others who feel the same way.

Bible Chapters

There was a time in my life that spanned several years that I would sit and conduct a channeled writing. A channeled writing is like taking dictation for me. I would just transcribe on paper the words that were being dictated in my head. Then I would later begin the arduous task of using google to look up information to see how accurate it was. I had a close friend that often shared in this task.

During one such channeled writings, my spirit friends referred to the Bible as a great workbook for the School of Life we were all attending. My friends in Spirit also indicated it had great teachings. The only problem was some of the chapters were missing, and it was difficult to learn the entire study program without the entire book. I was in shock. I had never heard such a thing in all my church studies. I immediately called my good friend Nancy. I asked her if she could verify this information since she was an ordained Methodist minister. She answered me quickly and said, "Yes, Kim, that is true." She went on to explain how that had occurred. At the time the Bible was written, organized religion decided which books would be included.

Unfortunately, all the metaphysical books and the books written by women were left out. A few weeks later, I attended a lecture by Gregg Braden who is an American author on consciousness, and he spoke of the Dead Sea Scrolls as well as other missing books of the Bible. That was a big aha for me. That same day, hours after listening to Gregg Braden, I heard again from my spirit friends say, "See, all is not as it appears." Years later, I would come to fully understand and appreciate that quotation and how it applied to the Bible and the missing chapters.

Bible

While the Bible is a great workbook for the School of Life, we need to keep in mind the time it was channeled to the prophets. What was going on in the world they lived in? Many of my loved ones and friends are strict in keeping with the old traditions and the exact teachings contained within. I often have reminded them that we no longer are sacrificing animals at the altar or offering burnt offerings. Often, I find we are picking and choosing only those things that fit. If the prophets of those times had written today, the writings would be much different and interpreted differently as well. The one thing that would not change is the disagreements between the believers and the non-believers and the difference of opinions between the religious factions.

I also have concluded that if God, Source, chose prophets at the time of the writing of the Bible, then why would God not choose prophets in today's times? After all, Jesus did say, "You can do all this and more." I have witnessed many examples of this. And what do the missing books of the Bible say? I hope in my lifetime these missing books resurface and are made available to the public. Until then, we all must use some common sense and discernment.

Heaven and Hell

Most people believe that heaven is way out there. It is above us, and we cannot reach it or access it. But in all reality, heaven is around you. It is sharing the same space that you reside within. The only thing that is different is the fact that the soul drops the physical body that it no longer needs or is useful. It serves as clothing for the soul in order to be in the physical world. Once the body is dropped, the soul's energetic pattern is quickened. The vibration is dramatically increased. Most mediums will also confirm that heaven is around you daily. Have you ever felt as if someone was breathing down your back? Or have you ever caught something out of the corner of your eye? Often, it is a loved one in the afterlife. Pay attention to your pets, they are sensitive to energy shifts and will sense when your loved ones are around you. You may see your pets looking off into the upper areas of a room. They will begin moving their heads and their eyes as if they are watching movement. They are sensing a shift in energy. Christmas time at my house can get a bit overcrowded. The spirit world loves a good party where our own moods and spirits are high and love is bountiful.

Hell, on the other hand, has been explained to me as this: It is your thoughts and emotions. Hell is of your own making based upon your thoughts and emotions. Upon death, you will go through a life review. During that review, you will experience and feel every emotion you have ever caused another. After all, this life is all about evolution, and that includes understanding how you have affected other people. It is not about what incident took place. It has to do with the thoughts and emotions the experience created. So, you will get to feel the good and the bad. I can only imagine how someone like Hitler felt. I have asked several times if I can bypass mine. The answer is always no. But at least I tried. I am not looking forward to the life review part when I think about some of the things I have done to others. When I have these thoughts, I am reminded of all the good I have done as well and how I have been a positive influence in others' lives. A life review is an overview of everything your life consisted of.

Your hell is self-imposed. If you start to think about your life and your disappointments, you will become extremely good at putting yourself in a self-imposed hell on earth. Most people already beat themselves up due to weight, looks, not enough money, et cetera. It is a broken record you continue to play in your mind. God, Source, loves you unconditionally and would never do that to you. God does not need to condemn you. You already got that move down all on your own.

Suicide

The first words out of Dawn's mouth during our first reading was, "Kim, if I kill myself, what will happen to my soul?" She had lost the love of her life a month earlier and had received my business information through a friend. I have never felt qualified to help people in readings who wish they themselves were dead. The grief they feel and are experiencing is unbearable. The only hope they have is for someone from the spirit world to show up and offer them comfort and guidance. All I can do is offer them hope and an understanding of the afterlife. I always encourage them to see a counselor, but most clients refuse. It's hard to explain to a counselor you wish your life was over without them locking you up or medicating you beyond being able to function. I have been there myself. Once you reach that mindset, you cannot see the possibility of the pain ending or a way out of your current circumstances.

I lost count a long time ago of the number of readings in which suicide was chosen by someone's loved one to facilitate their passing. The loved one in spirit always says the same thing. If they could go back and do things over again, they would. Their decision was a permanent fix to a short-term problem. They all wish they hadn't done what they did. The good news is there is no punishment for their actions. If they did not complete the lesson they were working on in this lifetime, no worries; they will return in the next lifetime and repeat again until the evolution lesson they were working on is completed. I often think about suicide. There was a time in my life I would beg the Spirit world to get me out of here. I wanted to go home, but then I know their answer, and as I look in the rearview mirror of my life, I think, "No, I am not cutting out early and coming back to go through all this crap again. I am staying to the end. I am going to learn this lesson one way or another." When I explain that to someone wishing to end their life, they choose to live and complete their lesson to the end as well.

Purgatory

Purgatory is referred to by the Catholics as a place of suffering the soul goes to until it has atoned for its sins before going to heaven. It is considered a place to cleanse your soul. I often have wondered what the process of atonement would consist of? The spirit world has always been adamant in disagreeing with this concept. There is a healing place that we can choose to go to if we had a difficult life or if we are in a self-imposed hell, but there is no holding place.

One day a few years ago, I was watching a special on TV regarding purgatory. The history of purgatory goes back to a time when suicide was occurring at an alarming rate. They did not have the embalming techniques we do today. So, in order to stop the daily suicide rate from climbing, the purgatory concept was pushed as a reminder to everyone what would occur if they took their own life. The general population was also reminded it was a sin to commit suicide as well. So, people were thinking twice about committing suicide. The purgatory explanation worked. It dramatically curbed the suicide rate.

If you think about it, why would the spirit world only have this special place for Catholics? Why not all the other religious organizations as well? And why not the Native Americans or the people living in the Amazon? It reminds me of being in a jail holding tank, sitting and waiting until you have spent a few hours in holding until you can be released back into society with everyone else, thus atoning for your actions. In all my experience, the afterlife is about love and compassion, not discipline and rules. To confirm this, I have conducted readings where a person committed suicide after murdering others, and their soul made their presence known within hours of the incident. They were raised as a catholic and even attended church right up to the altercation and their passing. No purgatory for them. Only love and compassion on the other side.

Spiritual Practices

There are so many different types of spiritual practices that are occurring and being practiced today. Not only do we have the ancient practices, but we have all the new-age forms of spirituality being brought to our attention and exhibited as well. The only thing that matters is if the practice is a form of love and service. Is it an opportunity to learn and evolve? Are you willing to be open to all possibilities for your development? If the practice is not destructive or selfish, then it is serving a purpose. Throughout my life, I have always had a huge interest in learning many forms of spirituality and divination systems. It is my hope and wish that people are tolerant and do not judge other's beliefs and spiritual practices. Eventually, we will all end up in the same place in the afterlife. We just took different roads to get there.

Take a moment to think of all the different forms of religions around the world. How did specific religious organizations get started? If you had grown up in the Amazon, what would your spiritual practice be? What if you grew up in India? Your beliefs and spiritual practices are more than likely directly linked to your upbringing as we discussed in Chapter 4. How have your views evolved over your lifetime regarding religious organizations and spirituality?

No Judgment

This is probably the biggest and most difficult lesson any soul must master. It divides the young from the old souls. I often tell people I have a long way to go in my evolution. I still catch myself forming opinions and making judgments about others. When my daughter began dating someone I disapproved of, I had to work on myself and question myself on how I developed my beliefs and expectations for my children. While I can see where the belief came from, it is so dang hard to change. I just have come to accept I am still a work in progress.

Living a life of unconditional love for all of mankind, the animal kingdom, and the plant kingdom is the ultimate test of all. Can you love unconditionally without judgment of another's religious beliefs and practices? If you are judging and thinking your way is best, then you are operating in a lower vibration energetically. The good news is, you are among good company. Approximately ninety percent of the population is right there with you. Eventually, everyone will evolve. It's just a matter of time and effort on your part. Remember, the spirit world does not have different religious organizations or practices. Man developed the religious organizations and the rules they follow and impose. The earth has been evolving for years, long before any structure of religious practices had officially been established. The other side keeps it simple. The only thing that matters is love.

As the quote by Dalai Lama at the beginning of this chapter states, "Just because someone is not on your road does not mean they are lost." Your childhood belief, life experience, and evolution level are what has determined the road you are on. Be kind to one another. You will all arrive home safe and sound no matter what.

~

Chapter 7:

You Have Spiritual Gifts

*"We could all be mediums and all have
absolute knowledge if the bright
light of our ego consciousness would not dim it."*

—Marie-Louise von Franz

The fourth step in the C.O.N.N.E.C.T.E.D. process is No Way
I Can Do This Like the Experts. In this chapter, you will
dispel myth three. You will learn that mediums, psychics, and
intuitives are not the only ones connected to the afterlife. We
are all connected. In this step, you will learn what the differences
are between each. You will also learn about your spiritual gifts
and soul evolution.

Back in 1993, my youngest daughter was born. I was a full-
time, stay-at-home mom. Once a week, I met two girlfriends
for coffee after dropping off the older children at school. It
was the one time during the week I had adult time. During
one such early morning coffee, I discovered something that
changed my perceptions about mediumship, intuition, and
psychic abilities. During a coffee get together, a conversation
began about a medium that had been on TV. One of my friends
remarked, "I wish I had his gifts." I asked her if she had voices

81

or thoughts in her head that she knew were not hers. Both of my friends looked at me as if I had gone off the deep end. They both answered at the same time, "No, never." I'm sure you can imagine where the conversation went from there. Before our early morning coffee get-together was over, I gave my girlfriend a reading in which her deceased grandfather appeared. At the time, I had no idea what I was doing. I had never officially developed, and the reading was disjointed and felt like I was reaching. But I can tell you it changed my girlfriend's life. She never forgot that reading and became one of my biggest fans, encouraging me to go forward with the ability I had been gifted with.

I tell this story because I honestly thought everyone could do what I do to some extent. It never occurred to me others did not have the same type of experiences I did. At the time of this coffee get-together, I had been searching and reading books on the subject. At that time, there were few books to be found. But this coffee had me pondering the thought, "Does everyone have spiritual gifts?" The answer should not surprise you. Yes, everyone has the gifts of spirit. After all, you are created as a spark of the divine made in the image of the divine. It is your birthright. It just depends on which spiritual gifts you were more gifted with.

Spiritual Gifts

Many of you never give a second thought to your unique talents and gifts. You use them every day, and they have become a secondary part of you. Some of you will become your gift and others of you will have more than one gift that becomes an outward expression of who you are, but everyone has the gifts of spirit to some degree. Being an artist, a singer, a musician, a healer, a counselor, animal whisperer are all gifts of spirit. Often, I would ask my spirit friends why I was never gifted with singing? As a child, I dreamed of standing on stage and singing. The answer was always the same; if you want to sing, you need to practice and develop that gift. The more I sang, the better I got. I even had solos in school concerts. But it never was a day in and day out driving force in my life like the mediumship.

I can only imagine how many hours Leonardo da Vinci practiced his craft. He lived it and breathed it every day of his life. It was probably his every waking thought until it became natural to him. It became part of him. Beethoven became an accomplished composer and pianist. He practiced and developed until he honed his craft. A young man who is autistic became the winner of America's Got Talent. That young man, Kodi Lee, not only is autistic but blind as well. Kodi is a great validation of how each person does have spiritual gifts. I would also bet he practiced and practiced and practiced.

You may not be a Leonardo da Vinci, Beethoven or Kodi Lee, but you can learn to develop if you are willing to put in the time and effort. It is up to you to what extent you develop your spiritual gifts based on how much time and effort you are willing to devote to learn it. For me, it has become my desire and hope to be the best I can be in order to serve spirit and to serve mankind. Therefore, I myself, devote endless hours to developing this gift and ability. It is something I enjoy and does not even seem like work to me.

Intuition

There are people who call themselves intuitives. They have developed their intuition to such a high degree that they are accurate when tuning into their gut feelings. Intuition is a gift that everyone has and can be developed. It is your internal GPS. Here is an example of how it works. You are driving to work one morning, and for some reason, you get a feeling to drive a different route than what you normally drive. You later hear on the radio that your normal route had an accident and is closed. That is your intuition at play. Most people just chalk it up to luck. Intuition will give you a sense of right and wrong or left and right, et cetera.

Psychic

Most people are confused about the difference between a psychic and a medium. What's most confusing is the fact that all mediums are psychic but not all psychics are mediums. A psychic will use the sitter's energy field in order to connect with the sitter and gain information about the sitter. They may use clairvoyance and telepathic skills. A psychic will often use a divination system or other method to obtain information. Divination systems include Tarot cards, runes, scrying, oracle cards, playing cards and bones to name just a few. A psychic reading may offer guidance, introspection, and strategies to overcome life's challenges. In a reading, it is one to one with the sitter and the psychic. All information picked up is directly connected to the sitter. The information is contained within their auric field.

Medium

A medium is a psychic and has the spiritual gifts to communicate with loved ones who have passed away. They use several techniques to communicate. There is a detailed explanation in Chapter 10 of the variety of ways the communication takes place and a detailed explanation of each. There are mental mediums, trance mediums, and physical mediums. I have been blessed with all three. It has taken me most of my life to accept it as not a curse. Although, some days, it still feels that way. There are also animal communicators as well who connect with animals who have passed.

Mental Medium

A mental medium uses their mind in order to communicate with the afterlife. Many people would use the term telepathic, and that would be true. Telepathy is used to convey words, symbols, numbers, and even a thought. Most mediums are mental mediums.

A word of caution in booking a reading with a medium. I have witnessed and experienced some over the top awesome readings, and I have also had readings in which the medium should not be doing readings at all. A good reading should consist of information that cannot be researched on Facebook or googled about the deceased person. Some internet information may come in, but there should always be pieces of evidence that are only known between the sitter and the person that passed away. I have had several clients tell me I told them something from their loved one that they never shared with another person.

I am still amazed at the number of times a sitter will answer no to something and later find out it was true. The loved one in spirit may also give specifics on something the sitter has to go research or ask another family member. I love it when that happens. I have concluded the information being relayed from the other side is more accurate than the information the sitter sitting in front of me provides. I have also had the spirit communicator relay a future event or happening. I think they will take the opportunity to make a skeptic a believer. They have also shared when a current family member has a health issue that should be addressed. There is no doubt in my mind they are sharing that information out of love and to validate it is them.

Trance Medium

A trance medium is also a mental medium. The medium will go into a trance state and let the spirit communicator speak through them. The best way to describe this is similar to taking dictation. The medium is speaking the words of the spirit communicator. I have always struggled with this form of mediumship. I have a strong feeling that most mediums calling themselves trance mediums are speaking from their own higher self and, in some instances, from a previous life they have lived.

I am the biggest skeptic there is. I want proof they are who they say they are. Without proof, a medium can often be portrayed to the public as a fraud. Many trance mediums don't understand this concept of proof. They just want the public to take them at face value and believe they have a spirit communicator. I have prided myself on bringing through spirit communicators that lived many years ago. They have no connection to a family member or friend connection with anyone in the circle I am sitting in at the time of the trance communication. I have had the spirit communicator give specific details that were later confirmed by another member of the group. It always gives me that big aha moment. Evidence and validation are key for me.

I have had the privilege of participating in a trance development circle with other very gifted trance mediums. It is not uncommon to witness clear and obvious phenomenon that takes place. I have witnessed lights changing colors, spirit faces captured on video, voices on videos, and other interesting and wonderful happenings. As I have stated before, being a skeptic, I appreciate the spirit world providing evidence for validation. It gives me confidence and proof the afterlife does exist.

Physical Medium

Physical mediumship involves the spirit communicator using the energies of the medium and producing effects that can be seen, witnessed, or heard by everyone in the room. This includes transfiguration, direct voice, apports, levitation, and materialization.

I have mixed feelings on this form of mediumship. On one hand, I love it. There is no denying what is taking place, and proof can be shown in the way of videos and pictures. For years, physical mediumship has been done in the dark or under dim red light. You can read several accounts in which the medium was tested. In today's times, unfortunately, there are many frauds claiming to be a physical medium, which makes it even more difficult for the public to be open-minded. The public also gets creeped out easily over this type of phenomenon. With no physical body, the spirit world needs to use other means to form an energetic body shape. That is what can be scary to some.

Soul Plan

It is possible to see exactly the areas of your spiritual gifts. Astrology, Cards of Destiny, and numerology can identify the areas of your strengths and spiritual gifts. Every gift can be developed to some degree. You will intuitively know your gifted areas based on your perception of it. Does it come easy for you? Do others praise you in certain areas of life? Is it something you love to do and get lost in time doing it? Do you have a sense of fulfillment and satisfaction? Spend some time and give it some thought in answering these questions. You will quickly see your gifts of spirit.

~

Chapter 8:

Mediumship 101

*"Whilst we can teach the mechanics of
mediumship, we must never forget that
mediumship is first and foremost
a spiritual and sacred act."*

—Martin Twycross

The fifth step in this C.O.N.N.E.C.T.E.D. process is *Education about Mediumship*. In this step, you will learn the inconsistencies of mediumship and how to interpret the meaning of each. You will learn to discern the difference between a guide providing you information and a loved one. This chapter includes many tips and areas requiring clarification that will help you with your mediumship development. At the end, you will understand some of the issues with mediumship and how to work around them.

Mary was a talented medium. She had been developing for years. I participated in an online circle with her for approximately two years. She was consistent and accurate. I aspired to be like her one day. I felt honored and privileged to be in her presence learning from her. She always had a way of making everyone feel special. She never judged anyone. She always encouraged us to stretch and reach higher. At the end of each circle, she would remind us of why we were learning to be a medium. In Mary's opinion, the only reason was for love and service of others, to bridge this world to the next in order to bring two hearts together once more.

Since those first classes with Mary, I have attended several other development circles and studied under many mediums who are also talented, but I never forgot Mary's wisdom. She was by far the sincerest teacher and mentor I have worked with. Maybe it was because my beliefs were in alignment with hers, and maybe it was because she was my first real teacher. I have always felt an indebtedness to the spirit world, my friends in spirit, and my loved ones in spirit. They have never let me down, and they have always shown up whenever I needed them. Even during a reading, they are there and on time.

This book is partly for the spirit world as well. Those in spirit are your loved ones, your family and your friends. They love you beyond words and want to connect and communicate with you. Before we go much further, there are some items, we need to clear up so you are not confused as you develop and progress further. These are the nuggets of gold I wish I had been taught in the beginning. They are areas that I stumbled over and had much difficulty with. I share these with you so you experience smooth sailing as you go forward.

Love Is the Key

There is much love on the other side. It is true that love never dies. It only gets stronger as we grow and evolve. There have been many times people wish they had told someone how much they loved them prior to their passing. Once they are gone, it is still not too late to tell them how you feel. Your loved ones do hear your thoughts. When desiring to connect with the other side, keep in mind the love you feel for them. Love, being the highest vibration there is, will go a long way in connecting with your loved ones. It is the key to life.

Service

There is a direct link to your loved ones who have transitioned to spirit through the power of love. It makes it much easier to connect because you automatically feel the love without forcing it to happen. But if you are reading this book in hopes of learning mediumship in order to do readings, then you must come from a place of service – service to the spirit world and service to your sitter. I ask nine out of ten days, "How can I be of service today?" "What can I do to make the world a better place?" Whenever I have a sitter in front of me, I ask my spirit friends, "How can I help this person to find peace, understanding, and purpose?" Being of service to both sides of the veil unlocks doors you couldn't dream of. You are putting others first, and that opens the heavens to you. It means you are coming from a place of unconditional love, and love is the highest form of service.

Live Not from the Ego

This is easy to say but hard to do. Seeing life through the soul's eyes takes practice. It is part of your evolutionary path. As you grow and expand over time, this will come naturally to you like riding a bike. But if you want to speed up your development, you can by looking at how you view certain aspects of your life. Take money, for example. Have you ever stolen money from another whether it be a family member, friend, employer, or neighbor? What was the reason you did it? Was it out of necessity or just because you felt an undeniable urge to do it? If you stole out of necessity, there would have been an underlying fear associated with it. You would have had a fear of lack of money. There is no law or rule against making money. Money is a form of energy we use in the physical world. The only thing that matters is how you acquired it. Using money as an exchange of energy is perfectly fine. If you are in an energetic agreement with another regarding a money exchange, then all is well spiritually. If you are not in agreement with another, then you are living a life where the ego is driving your car and the soul is the passenger which will take you farther away from your spiritual goals. The ego tends to live a life of selfishness, and it's all about "me." It will often resemble fears and lack whenever the ego is in charge. Younger and less developed souls tend to live a life where the ego is more dominant than the soul. Take a few moments before you go to bed each night and review your day. Who was driving your car?

Connection Is Within

The connection to the spirit world will be made from within your energetic pattern, your soul. Your soul is directly connected to the other side through your higher self. And your higher self has a direct connection to the entire universe. This includes all universal wisdom and knowledge. You are also connected to every soul, all animal souls, and all plant life as well. You can connect with everything once the soul is in an evolutionary state of alignment with Source, the Divine, or God, whatever reference you feel comfortable with. In order to connect with your loved ones, you will use this higher-self channel.

The easiest way to explain this is to imagine how you daydream. The daydream comes from within your mind. If I asked five people to picture being at a beach, each person would describe the picture they created in their mind differently. The spirit world will use this area of your consciousness in order to communicate pictures, symbols, numbers, and words.

Even your emotions and sensations such as goosebumps, sneezing, et cetera will also be utilized by your loved ones in spirit. They create this within your body even though you may see the effects on the outside. They will often use this technique as a calling card. I always know when my deceased father is present during a meditation as I will begin sneezing for no reason.

Results Are outside You

While the connection is made from within you, many of the results of the connection will appear in your outside surroundings. Just like the sneezing I referred to above. The sneezing is triggered within my body, but the actual sneeze is the outside result. You will need to become aware of your surroundings and the details that begin playing out in your day to day activities. If you begin paying close attention, you will begin to read between the lines and see the results of your connection to your loved ones manifesting in the physical world.

Guides

There is much that can be written about guides in the spirit world. Guides are similar in nature to a teacher. They are there to help keep you on task to learn what your soul intended to study in this lifetime. If you are reading this book, your soul is ready for you to move to the next level and learn another aspect of your existence. Just like you had a specific teacher who taught you English, you will have a specific guide who specializes in connecting to the afterlife.

I studied under a teacher in Chicago for two years. She did a variety of things. One area she spent a lot of time with was guides. One session I had with her, she said to me, "Your guide is ready to change out, and you are moving to another level with a new guide. Do they have your permission to switch guides?" Sure, I thought. I was secretly skeptical about the entire thing. My teacher asked me to sit quietly in a chair and to close my eyes and take some deep breaths. She started reciting and saying a verse of some sort. The next thing you know I saw a gentleman in a solid gold jester costume in my mind's eye. Even his hair and face were a beautiful gold. He came swooping in and bowed to me. He stretched out his arm and handed me a business card and stated to me, "Here is my calling card. I am at your service." He then laughed. How weird I thought.

The next day, I got up early and started packing for a holistic expo in Minnesota. I started to experience a strange sensation on my face. By the middle of the afternoon, I had some rash on my face. It resembled a bad case of rosacea. I had never had anything like it before. I said to my friend Marilyn who attends shows with me, "This is strange. I don't know what it is, and I hope my makeup covers it up." It was not painful. It was bumps all over my face.

The next day, we attended the holistic expo. Across from my booth was a spirit artist. She was approximately my age and had a pleasant demeanor. Over the course of the day, I kept looking at her. I couldn't quite put my finger on it, but I knew she was somehow an important piece to my journey.

The expo was two days in length. On Sunday at about noon, the pleasant spirit artist came over to my booth. She said she felt guided to draw a picture for me. By this time, I had already known there was something special about her. I told her I was happy to pay her to do one. Toward the end of the day, I stepped over to her booth to collect my drawing. As she handed it to me, she said, "This is your new guide. He told me to draw him in all gold. You will know why." I looked at the picture and it was the same gold gentleman in the jester costume handing me his calling card two days earlier. The spirit artist also told me, "Your face will clear up tomorrow. Your guide is sorry for the energy being too strong on the transfer of guides." I looked at her, and I'm sure my mouth dropped to the floor. I don't think I said two words for quite some time, and that is not like me. I was in shock and speechless. I relayed the entire story to her and thanked her.

The entire drive home, I remained in total shock. I arrived home and kept looking at the picture of the man in gold drawn by the spirit artist. She had nailed it. The next day when I awoke, my face was back to normal. The picture of my gold guide hangs in my reading room. His picture has earned its place in my reading room and in my heart. At the time, I thought guides changing out was a load of crap made up by my mentor. I needed the validation of what had taken place. I guess my guides knew it too and had to prove it in the only way they can – in a grand jester. Literally! I am now a believer in changing out guides, and no one will convince me of anything different.

Thinking back to your time in school, you may have fond memories of classmates, and you will also have memories you can't forget fast enough. This same concept is true for your soulmates. You are here to help each other learn, expand, and evolve.

Long before you arrived, your soul had a specific focus on what it desired to learn based on its evolution level. My ex-husband and I got together in the spirit world and agreed to help each other learn specific lessons and areas of study. I wanted to learn confidence, forgiveness, and to speak my truth. We discussed my goals and decided how I would achieve this and how he would help me. Our souls arrived, and we met on our journey in the physical world. We got married, and he cheated on me – not once but several times. We kept getting back together. Eventually, after nine times – yes, you read that correctly – we went our separate ways. I finally found the courage to speak up for myself.

Years later I studied numerology and Cards of Destiny. Both are systems that look at your life and what you came to do in this lifetime and how you came to do it, what your challenges are, any karmic debt, and the areas of life that will be easy for you. Interesting that when I studied both systems, I learned that the number nine is the number for completions and endings. I could see how there was a higher plan at play regarding my ex-husband.

Without his help, I would not be doing what I am today. I cannot thank him enough for helping me to learn these valuable lessons. I went on and married again. If I had not found my inner voice and confidence, I would not have met my current husband. Now I can see how my past marriage benefited my current place in life. Not only from a marriage position but from all future relationships I encounter.

I received an apology email from my ex-husband. I responded by telling him I had forgiven him years ago. On a deep soul level, we both know exactly what lessons were mastered from the entire experience we shared together. I know when we arrive back in the spirit world, we will show up in class together again and thank each other for committing to help each other learn these lessons that were painful at the time. These lessons, in the end, helped my evolution beyond words.

Time Frame after Death for Connection

When I first started to develop and learn mediumship, I attended spiritual development classes. In those classes, the teachers were adamant about not doing a reading until a minimum of six months had passed after someone transitioned to spirit. Apparently, someone at one time had taught the first mediums that it took time for us to get accustomed to our new home in the afterlife. I am surprised at how many mentors and teachers still teach this today. In my own experience, I learned quickly that is not always the case, and I had no control over when or who would show up in a reading.

Your loved ones will show up when they are ready and when you are ready for it to occur. The last thing your loved ones want is to put you through more pain and agony. My father passed away in 1986. It was twenty years later before he ever came through in a reading. Prior to that, I'm not sure I was ready for it. We were extremely close, and at the time he passed away, I went into a deep depression. If he had come through sooner, I know I would not have searched so frantically to develop my mediumship gifts. Knowing my dad, he probably hid out for that reason.

I have given readings and brought a deceased loved one through in which the sitter told me they were still alive, only to find out later their loved one had passed, and they were not aware of it at the time of the reading. I have concluded that our loved ones in spirit know what is best for us and what timing is best for us as well. I have learned to let go and trust that everything is happening as it should and as it was planned. I hope when I transition I come through and let my children know I am okay and I arrived home safe and sound. I have already told them I am stalking them until they acknowledge me.

Children

Many of the long practicing mediums do not believe in doing readings in which young children come through. I never have understood this belief other than the beliefs we as humans carry regarding minor children. It is fascinating to me how the older souls are trying to help the younger souls in developing and expanding. We see it carries over into the physical world as well with adults helping and protecting minors.

Do not confuse the age of the body with the age of the soul. The body is the set of clothing the soul is utilizing. It is possible to have an old soul occupying a child's body. If the child had lived into adulthood, you could have determined quickly how evolved their soul is. Whether they are a young soul or an old soul, love pushes them to connect with you again. I have seen all ages step forward to connect with their loved ones. Even infants can carry on a meaningful conversation with their loved ones they left behind. There is no physical body in spirit, only the soul with a strong desire to communicate out of love for you.

Alzheimer's and Dementia

This is one area that surprised me. Often during a reading, a loved one in spirit steps forward and the sitter told me that the spirit communicator I was picking up was still alive but in a nursing home with an extreme case of Alzheimer's or dementia. Their loved one I had connected to would give explicit detailed information that would and could be validated by the sitter. To me, it appeared as if they had already passed away. It was very confusing, to say the least.

What I have learned from my spirit friends is that both these illnesses allow you to have one foot in this world and one foot in the spirit world. While your body is here in the physical, your consciousness has already transitioned to the afterlife. It often helps to ease the transition process for both you and your loved ones.

It is important to note that as a mental medium, I shift my consciousness and awareness from the physical world to the spirit world every time I conduct a reading. In a way, I as well have a foot in both worlds. The only difference is I am very aware of what floor on the elevator I am exiting – the first floor being the physical earth and the second floor being the afterlife.

Missing People

Early this spring, my phone rang. I answered it, and on the other end of the line was Jacob's mother. She lived a few miles from me and was desperate to locate her missing son. Her son was nineteen years old and had been missing for over twenty-four hours. She conveyed to me it was not like her son to not come home and could I please help find him. My heart sank. I could not imagine as a parent the feeling and emotions this family was going through. Jacob's mother was willing to do anything to find her son. She loved him and wanted him home.

This was not the first call I had received regarding Jacob. This was the sixth. I had explained to all the previous callers it was not as easy as they thought. I did not go into an explanation as to why with each previous caller; I just declined my assistance. But Jacob's mother's call was different. It was different because not long into our conversation, Jacob's father joined our phone call. Our call quickly was moved to speaker for all of us to hear. My heart swelled, and I wanted nothing more than to help them.

For the next three days, I spoke to Jacob's father daily. I passed along everything I was picking up from Jacob. He was able to pass along specifics about the last evening he was alive, who he was with, and situations that occurred involving others. He provided landmarks close to his current location and that he was under water and close to his vehicle. Within a week, Jacob was located, and his body was returned to his family for a proper burial. His family could now find the peace they had been looking for. I was relieved as well. In my experience, many missing people are never recovered. Jacob's family was lucky. Their son was found at the bottom of a lake. In all reality, it may have taken months or years to locate him, and in the meantime, the family would have continued living in agony, never knowing and always wondering what happened to their one and only son.

A few months later, I received a call from Jacob's father. He thanked me for my help and apologized for not acknowledging me at his son's visitation. He explained how he was so distressed and barely able to function. We continued to have a conversation about life and death and some of the inner workings of my knowledge about the spirit world. It brought him comfort to know more about his son's passing.

I explained to Jacob's father how many years earlier I belonged to a mediumship group that worked with the police in locating missing people. It was extremely difficult for me as I see dead people as alive, and I see live people psychically as alive. It is hard to distinguish a difference. To locate someone is a process. As a psychic and medium, I try to backtrack as to who they were last with and where they were last seen or located. This can be done by using a system called remote viewing. Then I ask the spirit communicator to give more details such as road markings, street signs, et cetera. It can seem like pulling teeth. It is extremely difficult.

Many people don't understand that our essence is still who we are whether we are alive or passed. If they are ashamed of their passing, then they may not be ready to share what happened. If a loved one is involved in their passing, they may try and protect their loved one. It is not easy, and it is not cut and dry. There are groups that specialize in this. It takes time and practice in understanding this. For a psychic medium, they can pick up the essence of someone not only as a medium but psychically as well.

Pets

I attended a holistic expo in St. Cloud, Minnesota a few years ago. I was browsing in a booth when I kept hearing someone speaking to me telepathically. It was clear it was a psychic connection. I looked around and did not see anyone. Normally in my experience, I am looking around to see who I am connecting to. I looked down, and there sat a service dog staring at me. I asked, "Are you talking to me?" The next thing I knew the dog was conveying to me that he had been taking medication for his hips, and the pills had helped but the owner had stopped giving him the medication. He asked me to tell her, his owner, the pills were working and could he get them again.

By this time, there were approximately twenty people watching the connection between myself and the service dog. I told the owner what I was picking up from her service dog. She quickly confirmed everything and told me she was short on money, so she quit giving him the pills. After our conversation, she stated she would find the money and begin the medication again. This was a big *aha* for me. It was the first time I was able to confirm animal communication that even I believed.

It is not uncommon for me to pick up pets who have passed that have a direct connection to the sitter or the spirit communicator. If you are hoping to connect with a pet, it is possible to connect with them if they have transitioned to spirit, and it is possible to connect with them psychically. Love does amazing things.

Also, pay attention to your pets. They will typically let you know when your loved one is around. They will start to look upward into thin air. They will begin moving their heads as if they are tracking something moving in the thin air. Just so you know, they are tracking a loved one. When this occurs, close your eyes, take some deep breaths, and ask in your mind, "Who is here?" The first name that comes to your mind is the deceased loved one that is near. Thank them for coming. You can then ask them to confirm it is them by using one of the testing techniques in Chapter 12.

Holidays and Celebrations

One of the easiest times to pick up and sense your loved ones is during the holidays or a celebration. The energy we are emitting is of an extreme vibration during these times. We are experiencing joy, love, happiness, et cetera. Your loved ones in spirit are drawn to the higher vibrations. Therefore, pay attention to what you sense and feel during these times.

Masculine and Feminine Energies

Distinguishing between masculine and feminine energies can be confusing. When I sense a spirit, I also will sense either a feminine or masculine energy attached to the spirit communicator. From time to time, you will get it wrong. If a female was a tomboy when they were alive or had heavy masculine energy, they will have masculine qualities attached to them as a spirit communicator. If a male has feminine qualities, you will feel as if they were a female when they were alive. Because of this, I attempt to get validation in more than one way with the spirit communicator.

Grief, Joy, and Love

Many times, immediately after losing a loved one, you will feel
a deep sadness. This is a common feeling with everyone who
loses a loved one they cared about. You miss them immensely.
As in my case with the loss of my father, my sorrow turned
into depression. Depression is a mood disorder that is treated
as a medical illness. I could not snap out of it without medical
intervention.

If you are in extreme grief, it will be difficult to connect with
your loved ones. Grief acts as a cloud and fog making it difficult
to connect. The vibration is low and slow. Joy and love clear
the way, making it much easier to connect as the vibration of
happier emotions is much quicker and upbeat. Missing someone and feeling sorrow is one thing, but extreme depression is
something entirely different, requiring medical intervention.
Imagine the love you feel for them whenever you are trying to
connect with them.

You Are in Control

Always remember that you have the final say. It is a learning
process for both you and your loved ones in the afterlife and your
spirit guides. In the beginning stages of learning, the blending
process, I would have physical sensations of what happened
to the spirit communicator at the time of their passing. If they
had drowned, I would feel as if I had a hard time breathing or
catching my breath. One time, I had a spirit communicator
pass away from falling and hitting his head. I felt the whack
to the back of my head and had a physical headache for hours

afterward. Thank goodness I had a good teacher. She told me to tell the spirit communicator to back off. She said to tell them their energy is way too strong. I relayed what she said and added my two cents as well. I told the spirit world if they ever did that crap to me again, I was quitting with all readings. Needless to say, it never happened again.

You are always in control of your body and your mind. No one can ever take control of you. That is just plain crap if anyone ever tells you that or makes you feel fear in any way whatsoever. In learning this process, you will discover the rewards of developing far out weight the obstacles. Your loved ones want to connect because they love you, not because they want you to be afraid of them. They are learning how to do this as well. They are working with their own energy in a way that is new and unique to them. Sometimes, they can be a bit strong. It reminds me of telling my grandchildren to please use their indoor voice. Communication and practice are the keys. Tell your loved ones what you are feeling and sensing.

～

Chapter 9:

Meditation and Blending with Spirit

"All things share the same breath – the beast, the tree, the man. The air shares its spirit with all the life it supports."

—Chief Seattle

The sixth step in the C.O.N.N.E.C.T.E.D. process is Commingling Energies. In this step, you will learn the importance of meditation and learning to blend with spirit. You will be introduced to techniques to accomplish both. You will also gain an understanding of how implementing each in your daily rituals will help connect you with your loved ones in the afterlife.

When I began developing years ago, I often heard other mediums referring to the blending with spirit. It was confusing, and no one ever could explain the exact meaning of that phrase. I was always instructed to blend my energies with spirit's. "What the heck. Wasn't that what I had been doing all along?" I thought. It was even more confusing to be told to blend with spirit but also told to meditate. I thought they were one and the same.

Over time and my experience, I finally understood there is a definite difference.

Blending with Spirit

The process of blending with spirit is different from meditation. To blend with spirit, you become aware of the higher vibration taking place. You begin to feel the energy of spirit. You will feel the energy moving around you. I often feel a slight pressure on my crown area, and sometimes I can hear the buzzing of nothingness. I will get a spider-like feeling over my face, and I may feel like I want to scratch it. I may feel as if my face is on fire or extremely warm. Many times, I feel a slight energy shift, and my entire body becomes heavy, and I am unable to move my arms or my feet. I become super still. I have felt my heart begin to race, and when that happens, I tell the spirit world to back off. I have felt a shift in the temperature. Many times, the temperature will drop significantly, and it will get cold in the room you are in. If any of this happens and you are uncomfortable, tell the spirit world the energy is too much. Time seems to stand still when I am in the process of blending. I can sit for an hour, and it feels as if I sat for ten minutes.

Over time, I have become a junkie in blending with spirit. I love the feeling. I am addicted. It is like nothing else I have ever felt. Sitting and learning to blend with spirit is an important aspect of development, especially in developing your mediumship gifts. Your loved ones in spirit will use this tool in order to connect with you using physical means, such as goosebumps, sneezing, a touch of the cheek, et cetera. It is ever so slight a feeling, but with time and practice, you will begin to feel it. By sitting and blending, you are giving the spirit world the opportunity to blend their energy with your energy. It is how their thoughts become your thoughts and how they will send you images. They are working to have their energies become one with your energies. That is why it is called blending. They use this technique in order to connect with you and for you to learn how to connect with your loved ones as well.

You may begin to feel sensations that you have never felt before. Remember, you are always in control, and you can stop at any time. It is important that you communicate to your loved ones what you are feeling and if it is uncomfortable or not. The more you sit and blend, the more it feels natural to you.

In the beginning, I suggest you sit and blend for ten minutes at a time. Eventually, aim to build your sitting and blending time to between forty-five and sixty minutes. Sitting daily is ideal but is unrealistic in my life and probably in your life as well. I do make it a practice to sit once or twice a week. Sometimes I sit for thirty minutes, and sometimes I sit for an hour. I let the process unfold on its own.

Meditation

When you are meditating, you are shifting your awareness to your higher consciousness. It is to shift your awareness to the area where your imagination and daydreams take place. That is where your focus shifts. The key is to have an empty imagination, to go mentally blank. It means to step your mind away from the day to day thoughts. Relaxing the mind is your goal. Try attempting for one hour to have no thoughts. Impossible isn't it. If you have difficulty relaxing your mind, then your loved ones will find it difficult as well to get through your mind, thoughts, in order to connect and communicate. It would be like they were walking through a minefield. They need your mind to be blank so it is receptive. Meditation helps in teaching you to do this. That is why meditation is extremely important. It also helps to put you into a relaxed and receptive state.

Not only is meditation important in order to connect with your loved ones who have passed away, but it is also helpful in obtaining a clear connection with your guides as well. Meditation helps the mind to relax and therefore reduces stress and anxiety. It can help to reduce depression as well. All your negative thoughts reside within the mind. If you can develop a meditation practice, you will see the benefits pay off in your day to day life. You will develop the ability to let your mind go blank whenever a negative thought creeps into your consciousness. Therefore, it no longer affects you mentally or physically.

There are different types of meditations you can do. You will find many guided meditations on YouTube. Listening to instrumental music is also a form of meditation. Even simply sitting on a park bench in nature is a form of meditation. The key is to be in the moment. No thoughts of past or present; just an awareness of the now. Try to let your mind go blank – no thoughts whatsoever.

Again, it would be ideal to develop a daily meditation practice. Meditate whenever you can find the time. Thirty minutes is an optimal timeframe for meditation. Find a quiet place where you won't be disturbed by people. Turn off your phone and any other items that will disturb you. Meditation can be done sitting or lying down. If you are lying down, do not relax to the point of falling asleep. You are practicing relaxing the mind, not turning it off. Take several deep breaths in through your nose and out through your mouth. Begin to slow your breathing down and relax. Place your hands palms down on your thighs. Do not cross your legs. You want a steady flow of energy that does not get crossed up. Concentrate on your breath. It is the breath of life. Relax, relax, relax. Continue to concentrate on your breath. It will help you to let your mind go blank. Try this technique three to four times a week before going on to the next step listed below.

First Step in Connecting with Loved One

After spending a couple of months meditating and blending with spirit, you are ready to move to the next phase. Use the same procedure you use to meditate. Close your eyes. This time, imagine you see the doors to an elevator. You approach the elevator, and the doors open. You step inside and look for the button that says Loved Ones. You push the button, and the doors slowly close. You wait for a moment, and the elevator begins to rise. The elevator comes to a stop, and the doors open. You step off the elevator and look around. You see what appear to be your loved ones from afar. You mentally ask them to step closer so you can see them and communicate with them.

Take three deep breaths in through your nose and out through your mouth. Then in your mind, ask your loved ones to step forward so they are standing in front of you in order to connect with you. Be specific with whom you are calling forward to interact with you. Take three more deep breaths. Then in your mind, ask your loved one to step close to you so you can feel and sense them. Next, ask them to give you a sign that they are there with you. Pay attention to the response you get. You may feel goosebumps, you may feel a brush on your cheek, or you may feel a tingling in your hands. You may begin to sneeze or feel lightheaded. After your loved one gives you their calling card, ask them in your mind to step back. Wait a few seconds, and then repeat the process, asking them in your mind to give you the same sign again. Do this procedure three times.

If you find this difficult or you get no response, go back to the meditation techniques and the blending with spirit procedure. This will only work if your loved ones have been given the time to learn to blend with your energies so you can sense and feel their presence. Do not skip or rush the steps. They are extremely important in your development, and they are extremely important for your loved ones in the afterlife. It does take practice and persistence. You are both learning how to connect with each other. There is no reason to rush the process so be patient. Your goal is to obtain success in establishing a connection.

If you do not like the elevator technique, then you can imagine riding an escalator and use the same steps when you arrive at the top. Imagine you are in an area surrounded by your loved ones in spirit. Then go through the same technique as the elevator.

The entire process of learning to blend with spirit and learning to meditate opens the doors and is a crucial step in connecting to your loved ones. The first time I realized I could connect with my father again using these techniques, I cried. I knew he was still there and was close to me. I could feel him. Your loved ones are there for you as well. Love has no limits on what it can do.

$\sim$

Chapter 10

The Language of Souls

*"If we would just take a moment to look
around, we would find that
the universe is in constant
communication with us."*

—Alexandria Hotmer

The seventh step in the C.O.N.N.E.C.T.E.D. process is The Language of Souls. In this step, you will learn the language your loved ones use in order to communicate with you. You will learn how they use symbols and how the clairs are used in communication.

Susan was a counselor. She lost her husband to suicide when she was twenty-eight years old. She was left with a two-year-old son to raise alone. She never dreamed life would go in the direction it did. Thirty-five years have passed since she lost the love of her life. Her son is an adult, married, and has a family of his own. She not only learned to survive, but Susan has learned to find happiness and to help others as well.

It was a beautiful summer day when Susan and I met at her home for a reading. As we sat on her large wooden deck overlooking the lake, the wind blew gently. The large oak trees provided shade from the hot sun, and the leaves on the trees danced in the wind. I looked at her and marveled. I felt I was being touched by the hand of spirit. I asked her if she felt the same. Susan smiled and shook her head yes as she said out loud, "Yes."

I could see her mind wander as she reflected on her past. She agreed with me. This home was special. After her husband passed away so tragically and unexpectedly, she wanted to make a change in her life. She wanted to start over. She had found herself in a situation that was unbearable. The only thing at the time that gave her and her son peace was time by the lake. They often visited a park with a beach on a beautiful lake. They both loved the water. Shortly after her husband passed away, Susan visited her accountant and asked him if she could afford a lake home. He assured her she could, and so she bought the home she now lives in. She raised her only son there and is currently following her dreams.

Susan loves to research her ancestry. She has been blessed to travel the world and study different cultures. She has booked several readings with me to learn about her past lives and to receive information from her loved ones in spirit about her current life and her past ancestors. She is following the bread-crumbs being dropped for her. Susan loves it. Through all her travels, she has also learned and experienced some of the unique languages and cultures from around the world. As time goes on, she is starting to see that languages are beginning to overlap from one country to the next.

Susan's story is a direct reflection of what is occurring with spirit communication. It does not matter where you live in the world. When you pass away, you will return to the Land of the Souls, and there, you will speak a language that is unique to all souls who have journeyed home. As the earth has progressed and we have evolved, we are starting to see more and more psychic mediums. The language barrier between our world and the spirit world is beginning to collapse. We are witnessing the overlapping of the language between our loved ones in spirit and our physical world. Both sides of the veil are wanting to connect in record numbers. How exciting for all of us.

I have been studying most of my life to learn the language of the souls. I know I could learn quicker if I traveled to this distant place. However, I'm hoping not to pay the travel fare any time soon. My knowledge has come from studying, practice, and trial and error. What I have learned I wish to share with you. It does take time and practice so do not give up.

The Connection

The connection will be produced in a variety of ways. I will list the most common ways the connection takes place. You have been preparing yourself by blending with spirit and meditating. Now we shall move to the next step. Your loved ones will utilize all your senses in order to communicate. It is up to you to pay attention to the information being provided. The information will come in fast and fade quickly. In the beginning, I kept a journal. I had difficulty making sense of what I was picking up. As time went on, I learned bits and pieces and the puzzle pieces started to fit together. I encourage you to keep a journal as well.

The connection will be different for each person. What works for one person may not work for another. It will be trial and error for each of you. Also, it is important to remember that your loved ones in spirit play an important role as well. They must relearn how to connect with you. They are now in a new land and now speak a new language. Their personality will remain the same. I find if they were chatty Cathy while they were alive, they will still be chatty Cathy on the other side. The essence of their souls and what is in their hearts will always remain. Their memories are also very much intact.

Clairvoyance

The most common gift used is clairvoyance also known as clear seeing. It is the ability to see visions either with your mind's eye or with your physical eyes. Your mind's eye is the area that you mentally receive images. It is very similar to the area of your imagination. Your loved ones will provide images of symbols, numbers, months, letters, colors, objects, and the actual spirit. This includes seeing auras as well in your mind's eye. I am often shown a birthday cake and streamers when someone's birthday is close. If the spirit communicator smoked, I will see the cigarette and smoke. All this is done in the area of my mind that images are created.

Every person living has an aura. An aura is often described as an electromagnetic energy field that surrounds people. It encompasses the body. Over time, I have learned to see the colors that are prominent in a person's energy field. For example, if I see green around a sitter in their energy field, I know they are a healer at heart. If I see blue in their energy field, I know they are a teacher and a good communicator. Yellow for me is the color of the intellect. I know they are very intellectual and grounded. Over time and practice, you will develop your own meanings to seeing auras around people. If you slightly close your eyes, then turn your head to the side and softly glance at someone out of the corner of your eye, you can often see their aura. There is much more to this short explanation. I could go on even regarding illnesses and the auras, but for now, just practice looking and seeing what you can pick up.

I often feel like the spirit world has chosen me as an ambassador for readings with skeptics and new sitters who have never experienced a reading. One such reading occurred a few years ago in Davenport, Iowa at a paranormal expo I was attending. An older woman close to my age (not telling) and a young girl sat down together for a reading. The young lady appeared to be close to my daughter's age. The reading began, and I immediately brought through a young man who was the older woman's son. He wished his mom a happy birthday and said hello to the young lady. Immediately, the young lady bolted from her chair and went running down the aisle. I looked at Marilyn who works for me and often accompanies me to my shows. We exchanged glances as if to say, "What the heck?"

I turned to the older lady and continued with the reading. Within a couple of minutes, the young lady returned with a young man close to her age. The young man looked a little rough around the edges as if life had been difficult. The young lady told the young man to sit in her now vacant chair. He sat, and I said, "Hello." Immediately, the young man in spirit said, "Hello, Bro. It's me." The spirit communicator then went on to show me how he hung himself and the item he used for his hanging. He continued to explain how his brother now sitting in front of me had found him and took him off the hook. The spirit communicator wanted me to explain the gory details to his brother, including the item he used for his hanging. I started arguing with the spirit communicator that it was not cool to do that to his brother or mother. The spirit communicator insisted and relayed to me his brother was a skeptic and would not believe me if I didn't tell him exactly how he passed, including every detail.

I took a deep breath and began to explain to the young man what his brother had just conveyed to me. I asked them all if they were okay with me explaining what happened to her son and his brother. They both agreed. So, I explained the entire play by play account of his passing. His brother who had just sat down looked astonished and put his head down and sobbed. Both brothers had spent time in prison, and both had recently been released from prison. The young man who passed away had recently lost his parental rights and decided to end his life. He went on to tell his brother to get his crap together. He could still turn his life around and make something of it.

That reading changed that young man's life. His brother in spirit used my clairvoyance in order to make his point to his brother who was still alive. He needed to make a huge impact on his life, and the amazing thing is, it worked. The young man still comes to get a reading when I am back in Davenport, Iowa, each year. He told me he needed to know the details of his brother's passing to make sure I wasn't a fraud. I'm happy to say he listened to his brother and is married with children. He now looks at life much differently. His brother's love from the afterlife created a miracle in his life and saved him from the path of destruction he was on.

It is not uncommon to see the method of the spirit communicator's passing clairvoyantly. I have been shown just about every manner of death imaginable. Your loved ones do not see death as we do. They look at death as a matter of fact incident.

They will use the images of their passing to prove it is them and to show their passing was not difficult in order to give you peace regarding it as in the above story. I have learned to not take anything personally. I imagine I am just watching a movie play out. Your loved ones have gotten good at using the area of your mind where daydreams and your imagination occur in creating images that appear real. I don't think I will ever stop feeling a sense of wonderment.

Clairsentience

Clairsentience is known as clear feeling. It is the ability to perceive information through your feelings and emotions. You may feel the love that they felt for you. You may feel as if you are drunk if they had been drinking. It is always a weird feeling when they do that. If they had felt depressed before they passed, you may feel depressed and sad.

Clairaudient

Clairaudient is known as clear hearing. It is the ability to hear words and sounds from the spirit world. These sounds can be presented to you in two ways. The sounds may come as a song playing in your head, for example. No one else can hear it but you. Or the sounds may seem as if they are happening in the outside world, but they are really happening in your head. I have been lying in my recliner resting when I hear someone say something. I looked at my husband and asked him if he heard that. He has always replied no. These sounds are in my head. This is the first way they will present sounds.

The second way they will present sounds is when everyone can hear the sound when you are together. There are times during readings when sitters are present, and we all hear tapping, or we may hear something falling off a shelf. Pay attention to the sounds going on around you. In the trance development circle I participate in, we have heard someone speaking when we play the recording back. All of us can hear the words spoken.

Clairgustance

Clairgustance is known as clear tasting. I remember one time during a reading when I had a taste in my mouth of tequila. I knew that taste right away and asked the sitter if the spirit communicator liked tequila. I was told yes. This rarely happens for me, but it does happen from time to time.

Clairscent

Clairscent is known as clear smelling. It is when you smell a distinct smell such as flowers, bread cooking, cologne or fresh-cut grass as examples. This is a common occurrence for many people.

Clairtangency

Clairtangency is known as clear touching. It is more commonly known as psychometry. By holding an object such as a watch or piece of jewelry, you will perceive information directly connected to the object and the person it belonged to.

Past and Future

Debbie attended an expo in which she had her first reading ever. During her reading, I told her I seen a baby coming in her family. Debbie informed me she only had one daughter, and her daughter had a medical condition that prevented her from conceiving. I went back and checked with my spirit guide in the spirit world and again told Debbie my guide was confirming a baby was coming in her family. I told Debbie I did not know how, but a baby was coming. I have learned to trust the spirit world more than I trust the sitters.

Approximately three months later, I received a message from Hailey. She was Debbie's daughter. She told me her entire family thought I was a fraud after her mother's reading. But her family, in the end, had to take back what they had said about me. Hailey had just found out she and her husband were expecting a baby. They went back and counted the days and figured she conceived five days after her mother's reading. The entire family was over the moon with joy and happiness and extremely surprised to say the least.

I often think the spirit world likes to have the last laugh. They will often do things such as Hailey and Debbie's story to make skeptics believers. The fact that this was Debbie's first reading ever, the spirit world took this opportunity to prove they do exist. I always love it when this happens.

There is no time in the afterlife. Our physical world has clocks, months, weeks, and years we follow. Information provided by the spirit communicator can be a memory or a future event you will experience in your life. At the time the information is being provided, you may not know or understand how the information fits. However, if I have come to learn nothing else, I have learned to trust the information and the fact it will eventually make sense.

Combining the Clairs

As you progress in your development, it is common for your loved ones in spirit and your spirit guides to combine the above clairs, especially if the blending process is extremely good. This happens when you are persistent and practice, practice, practice.

So you understand, I will share a reading that illustrates this process well. Stacy was a beautiful young woman in her thirties. She had recently lost the love of her life. During the reading, her boyfriend immediately came through. I saw him, and the next thing I knew I was in a car driving fast. It was nighttime, and the headlights were shining on the road. I knew I was driving on a less frequently traveled road. I was the one behind the wheel. I looked down at the speedometer, and I was in an old car that had the needle and speed gauge. The needle was as high as it could go showing I was traveling at a speed of more than 120 mph. All of a sudden, a deer ran out in front of me. I immediately took the steering wheel and swerved to miss it. My front wheel dropped off the edge of the road and the car rolled down a huge embankment. I could hear the glass break, and I could feel being tossed around in the car. I did not have a seat belt on. Everything occurred in slow motion.

The car came to a stop on its roof. I laid outside the car but within a few feet of it. Everything came to a dead silence. It was pitch black outside, but the headlights to the car were still on. I lay still and could hear the water moving in a nearby creek.

It was cool outside, and I felt cold. I could hear a car passing by at the top of the embankment on the road I was just on. It did not stop. Soon after I heard another car, I woke up, and I was standing over my body. I was confused. Then the entire replay goes through my mind, and I remember everything that just occurred.

Stacy confirmed everything I was shown. Her boyfriend restored old cars. He was driving a 69 Mustang at the time of his passing. The accident happened at night and his car laid at the bottom of a deep ravine by a creek. The ravine was so deep that it took two days before he was found. Lots of people showed up to search for him. Stacy said it was not like him to disappear. Eventually, he was located. His loved ones felt closure with finding him but always wondered what happened.

That is a good example of how the spirit communicator combined several clairs in order to connect with his girlfriend and to convey to me what had happened to him at the time he passed away. It felt as if it was happening to me. The blending process can be that good. Stacy was relieved to know what happened to her boyfriend. The entire family was at peace at last just knowing the cause of the accident.

∼

Chapter 11

Your Toolbox

*"Divination modalities heighten
your intuitive skills
Helping you recognize the magic
of meaningful coincidences."*

The eighth step in the C.O.N.N.E.C.T.E.D. process is Experience Different Modalities. In this step, you will be introduced to a variety of modalities used in connecting with your loved ones. You will learn how synchronicity works and how to recognize a visitation dream.

I was invited to a slumber party when I was in fifth grade. My girlfriend Cindy had invited eight of her closest friends to help her celebrate her birthday. In those days, it was common to have sleepovers with your friends. We would see who could stay up the latest. It just so happened at this sleepover Cindy's family owned a Ouija board. Cindy made it clear we could not use it while her parents were still awake.

We all waited until the chimes on the grandfather clock struck midnight. For some reason, we thought that midnight would open a portal to the other side. Cindy placed the Ouija board on the carpeted floor, and we all proceeded to sit around the board with our legs crossed on the floor. The lights in the room were dim. Cindy began reading a prayer from the directions that were included in the Ouija storage box. We then decided which two of us would use the Ouija board first. It was decided that Cindy and Ally would go first. Cindy was the only one out of the eight of us that had any experience with it, so it only made sense that she would be one of the two. Cindy placed the pointer on the Ouija board. I watched as Cindy and Ally then placed their fingers ever so lightly on the pointer. We all watched in anticipation. I could feel my heart racing and I could feel the other girls' energy as well.

Almost immediately the pointer began moving. First, an H and then an E. The pointer continued moving to L, L, and O. It had spelled the word hello. We were excited but also a bit apprehensive. The communication continued. Cathy grabbed some paper and began writing the letters down. The letters were G, R, A, N, D, M, A. We were in shock. Ally had lost her grandma a couple of years earlier. Then the craziest thing happened. The room went cold. Cold. We all looked at each other and were freaking out. It had become a scene from a Halloween movie. That ended our Ouija board experience. Suffice to say none of us slept the rest of the night.

That was my first experience with any form of divination modalities. After years of study, I can look back and smile at our adventure with a Ouija board. Since that encounter with a Ouija board, I have experienced the room going cold many times when sitting for physical mediumship or trance mediumship. It is what I refer to as a calling card from the spirit who is present. It no longer scares me. If anything, I love it when it happens. It is a validation for me that someone from the spirit world is present. And me being one of the biggest skeptics there is, I need validation all the time.

As with the Ouija board sleepover, your loved ones in the afterlife are trying to get your attention quite frequently. I now see that Ally's grandma was trying to give a message to her granddaughter, but we all just freaked out. My heart goes out to her grandma today. She had tried, but unfortunately, we were not open to receive. We shut her out, and we shut down the entire form of communication she was utilizing.

I am not suggesting you go out and purchase a Ouija board, but I am suggesting that in order to see the signs your loved ones are leaving, you must be open to all possibilities. If you can reach that level of understanding and awareness, synchronicities will begin showing up in your life as if by magic.

In this chapter, I am going to go over a variety of ways meaningful coincidences appear. The spirit world is always communicating with you. At times, it may be coming from your guide, and at other times, it may be coming from a loved one. You will know the difference based on what is taking place in your life, the timing, and the actual synchronicity. As we go through each one, I will give some examples and help you determine in the future if it is a guide or a loved one.

Feathers

You may find a feather in the oddest places. If you were brought up in a Christian home, you may associate white feathers with angels. Angelic beings are connected to the afterlife. Therefore, it only makes sense that your loved ones would use this symbol to communicate with you. You may quickly make the mental connection to heaven. You will know if it is from your loved one if they are the first person you think of upon finding a feather. Remember, they are also trying to contact you tele-pathically as well.

On the other hand, if you find a large feather from a raven or an eagle and your first thought is not of a deceased loved one, then the feather carries a message from your guide. Pay attention to what your thoughts have been focused on for the past twenty-four hours. Look up the spiritual meaning of that exact feather and see how it fits with the thoughts you have been focusing on. It is one of the many ways your guides are trying to help you.

Dreams

My ex-brother-in-law passed away a couple of years ago from esophageal cancer. A few days after he passed away, he appeared in my dream and said to me, "I made it, shoes and all." As he was standing in front of me, he picked up one foot at a time and showed me his pristine white tennis shoes. The shoes were pure white and looked brand new. Upon waking, the dream felt real to me. I knew right away he had visited me.

I never shared this dream with my older sister, as she is adamant about her beliefs and does not believe in what I do. However, I did have the opportunity to share my dream with my younger sister. A few days later after sharing my dream, I received a telephone call from her. I could tell she was extremely excited. She, her son, and his friend traveled to my ex-brother-in-law's funeral in support of him and his son, my nephew. They live in Oklahoma City, Oklahoma, and my older sister and her family live in Fort Worth, Texas. Over the years, they made this trip often for holidays and to just visit family. My ex-brother-in-law was loved by my entire family.

During the funeral, the minister spoke about my ex-brother-in-law's life and his family. The minister also spoke about some of the oddities in life that my ex-brother-in-law had, one of which was wearing his tennis shoes in the house. He could never go anywhere without his clean white tennis shoes. I could tell my sister was overjoyed to tell me the story. It helped both of us know he was safe and sound in the afterlife.

It is common for a deceased loved one to appear in your dreams. When you are asleep, you are physically and mentally relaxed. It is easy for them to telepathically connect when you are open and receptive. It will feel real to you, and honestly, it is. Thank them for entering your dream. If you want to try this technique, it works best if you do not go to bed overly tired or take any form of medication. Ask them to please come to you in your dreams, and if you are lucky enough for a visitation, thank them. It takes a lot of energy to make it happen on their end.

Dreams are also a great way for your guides to work with you. I studied dream interpretation for two years. I took classes and read several books. There are different types of dreams, and it would take another book to explain them. But if your guides are working with you to teach in a dream, you will remember the dream years later as if it just happened. Typically, these types of dreams are rare, but they do happen, especially if there is something you need to hear or learn.

Your higher self knows the symbols and how to apply them. It is your everyday waking self that gets confused about the meanings. Your guides and loved ones would appreciate it if you find one dream book and stick to the meanings of that book. Once you commit and tell them, okay, I'm going to use this dream book, they will start sending you messages that you can look up quickly and easily. If you use several books with several different meanings for symbols, it makes it difficult for your loved ones and guides to convey messages to you. Not only is it confusing for you, but it is confusing for them as well.

Journal your dreams and take the time to understand the meaning. You will begin to see the bigger picture. It is also one of the many ways you are connected on a higher level to the spirit world. Messages are being sent to you frequently. If you start looking up your dream meanings, you will be amazed at how dreams work.

Birds and Butterflies

Birds and butterflies both have wings and can move easily while in flight. Many people think their loved one has inhabited the bird or butterfly. The reality is your loved one has influenced their movement through their consciousness. It is interesting to note that the cardinal spirit animal is known to be a spiritual messenger because you become aware of having a spiritual connection. The butterfly spirit animal represents spiritual rebirth. They are representative of life. Many cultures associate the butterfly with our souls. Christians see the butterfly as a symbol of resurrection. Why wouldn't your loved ones send birds and butterflies with these profound spiritual meanings?

Numbers

Your loved ones will often use numbers to communicate with you. There are many meanings to numbers if you google angel numbers or spiritual number meanings. The specific numbers you should watch for have to do with specific dates connected to your loved one in the afterlife or you directly.

For example, if your loved one's birthday is September 28, you may look at the clock and see 9:28 either a.m. or p.m. If their wedding anniversary was March 16, then you may look at the clock at 3:16 p.m. or a.m. Pay attention to license plate numbers, the time you receive text messages, et cetera. The numbers will be unique to your loved ones in spirit.

Your guides will also use numbers to send messages. If your guide is aware of you looking up the spiritual meaning of numbers, they will continue to send you messages through numbers. Start paying attention if you see a repeating number. If it is not unique to a loved one, look up the meaning. You may be surprised at how well the message fits your current life.

Coins

My father passed away in 1986. I get messages from time to time, but one of the most profound messages came in the way of a penny. In 2014, my husband and I moved into a temporary apartment. We had not been in the apartment long when I moved a heavy chair to vacuum. There beneath the chair lay a single penny. I picked it up and looked at the year. The year was 1986. Not only was the year important, but I found the penny on my father's birthday. Finding the penny was a surprise. I was elated.

Whenever you find a coin, look at the year, and see if it connects to anyone that has passed away. If the year does not connect with anyone, reflect on what you were thinking about when you found it. And lastly, does the day have any significant meaning? Coins of all denominations are used by your loved ones.

Your guides will also leave you a coin or bills from time to time. Recently, I was having a difficult day. I was starting to question everything I was doing and the meaning of life itself when there on the ground lay a dollar bill. I picked it up and circled on the bill was In God We Trust. I got the message loud and clear.

Songs

Songs are often used by your loved ones. It is not uncommon to turn on the radio and your loved one's favorite song is playing. You will either hear the song on an actual radio or sound system, or the spirit world will play them in your head. Have you ever had a song start playing in your mind for no apparent reason? You may just start humming a song. When that occurs, ask yourself who has passed away that is connected to the song? Is there significance to the words and a connection to your loved ones who are alive or a loved one in the afterlife? Or is there a significance to the song and your current life and what is going on in your life? Pay attention, and you will know if it is a loved one or a guide trying to get you a message. And perhaps you had just heard it play on the radio an hour earlier so there is no connection to your loved ones or guides at all. You are just replaying in your mind a previous event.

Fragrances

You may recognize a perfume, a cooking smell, or cigar that reminds you of your loved ones. The smell may come out of the blue with no logical explanation, but it reminds you of a specific loved one.

Electrical Appliances or Equipment

John and Marsha came to see me for a reading late one afternoon. John had lost his best friend a few months earlier. They had a relationship as boss and employee as well as friends. Marsha also knew John's boss well. They had kids the same ages and had all grown up in the same small Iowa town. During the reading, Mike, who had passed away, kept handing me the remote control to a TV. I asked John and Marsha if this made sense to them and they replied no. In my experience, if a sitter cannot make sense of the information, it is only a matter of time when they do make sense of it.

An hour after the reading, I received a text from Marsha. When she and John arrived home, their fourteen-year-old son was standing at the door with two TV remotes in his hands. Neither one worked. We all got a good laugh. John told me at his next reading that it would be just like Mike to mess with the remotes.

It is not uncommon to have lights flicker and lightbulbs burn out. Anything electrical can be affected. You will know it is your loved ones if the occurrence seems odd to you and you make a mental note of the rarity of the incident.

Divination Modalities

Divination is a practice that can be used to foresee or foretell future events. It is a system or modality that you can utilize to ask the spirit world, your guides, for guidance and knowledge. The system works well if everyone involved stays on their current course. Life is fluid, and free will always has the last say in the end. The more people involved, the more difficult to predict a future outcome. There is no exact science to reading the energies.

In my experience, readings are most accurate if the reader has no emotional connection to the outcome of the question. If I try to read for myself or a direct family member, I feel I am blind and have no spiritual gifts or ability. We need to live our lives and participate in this physical life. Therefore, the natural laws of the universe kick in and keep me blind. So, if you're are trying to use any divination system for your life or a close family member, you will probably be blind as well, but if you are using it to be of service to another, it becomes a magical experience.

There are several modalities and systems utilized by intuitives, psychics, and mediums to give readings. I often see these systems as a springboard to connect with the spirit world. I have spent the better part of thirty years learning and studying several systems and modalities in order to find the one I deemed the most accurate. In the end, I learned all systems are accurate to some degree. The real accuracy comes from the person using the system. It depends on how developed the person is that is conducting the reading. Below, I am listing a few of the areas of study I have focused on.

Card Systems

Until I started researching card systems, I had no idea how many card divination systems existed. I have studied Tarot, Lenormand, Sibilla, Gypsy cards, Petit Etteilla, Psycards, playing cards, Le Grand Jeu, Tea cards, and Oracle cards. Each system has pros and cons. Some are super easy to learn. If you want to start with an easy system, I would suggest getting a deck of Oracle cards. Pick a deck that you feel drawn to. I do have a couple of card designers I like but usually not on one specific deck. There are three decks I use all the time.

Pendulum

You can make your own pendulum. All it takes is an object with some weight hanging on a string. You can ask yes and no questions. However, the pendulum will at times tell you it is not the right time to know the answer. Again, I have learned if I have an emotional tie to the outcome, my energy does influence the pendulum, so now I only ask questions that I have no desired outcome.

Numerology

Numerology is a great system to study if you are desiring to know more about your life purpose and how you will operate in this life. Numerology will give you timeframes that you can see and tell you how it will affect your life. Your soul came into this existence with a specific purpose in mind, goals it wanted to accomplish and lessons it wanted to learn. You have set up challenges, and most of you have karma to pay off. A numerology report will supply all this information.

Astrology

Astrology is the study of the planets, sun, and moon, how their positions and movements have a direct influence on your day to day life and relationships. It will help you to see the areas that will be a struggle and the areas that will come natural and easy for you. I have studied this for a long time and do find it difficult to understand. Evolutionary astrology is the area of astrology I find most fascinating and resonate with. If you research astrology, you will find there are several areas and branches of astrology.

Human Design

Human Design is a system that incorporates astrology, I Ching, Kabbalah, and the chakra system. In Human Design, you study a body graph to reveal your genetic design and how you respond to the world. This system helps you to understand the conscious and unconscious aspects of yourself.

Gene Keys

Richard Rudd is the founder of the Gene Keys system. He is gifted in metaphysical teachings. This system uses astrology and an archetypal understanding to compile your unique blueprint.

This blueprint tells you who you are, how you operate, and above all, why you are here.

Cards of Destiny

This system I came across in the last two years. I attended a holistic expo in which I lectured on numerology. After the lecture, an older gentleman approached me and said he drove two hours to speak to me. He came across my lecture on the internet by happenstance. He went on to tell me he has become much better at listening to his intuition. We laughed. I could relate to his statement. So, this time, he listened, and he drove to the expo, attended my lecture, and dropped by my booth to speak with me. He went on to explain that he was an author and wrote a book called The God Clock.

Needless to say, I was fascinated by his story. I, being the biggest skeptic there is, need to have something or someone drop on my head for me to listen. And this man piqued my interest, and his story was extremely intriguing. I listened to his explanation of the system, took his business card, and immediately went on the internet to order his books. After reading his books, I was inspired and quickly booked a reading with him. I was mesmerized by the reading I received.

At the time I ordered his books on the internet, I came across another author with the same system. I followed my intuition and ordered a couple of his books as well. Within a couple of months, I booked a reading with him as well. Again, I was blown away by the reading. You guessed it. I ordered every book written on this system, studied the system, and learned it. I now use this system to do readings as well.

The reason I like this system is that it incorporates astrology with a deck of playing cards. Numerology is used as well to track cycles and seasons in our lives. It shows what is capable in your life if you play your cards right. There is a higher side and a lower side to all possibilities. It is probably the most accurate of any system I have studied to date. And I have been searching, studying, and learning just about every system developed. This system also incorporates other people that are important in your life and what part they play in your reading. Relationships in this life are everything.

Destiny of Cards is a system that gives a layout of your entire life from birth forward. There is a lot to the system, and it does take some knowledge of astrology and numerology. I love this system. It did show I would have the opportunity and the energies would be right over a three-year time frame to write a book. Apparently, it is accurate about that.

The older gentleman that appeared at my booth one spring day was divinely guided. I could see it then, and I can see it now. I was guided to learn this system in order to help others and myself. There are things that happen in your life that are undeniable.

Meaningful Coincidences and Synchronicities

Your life is filled with synchronicities every day. You are always connected to the spirit world and your loved ones whether you realize it or not. On one hand, it may appear things randomly happen, but if you look closer at the details, you will see this is not the case. For example, why do apple trees produce apples and not pears? Why do trees grow with their roots seeking water to survive? What valuable lesson would you learn about fire if you were burned? Life may seem chaotic and random, but everything is orchestrated by you and your soulmates long before you arrived. Everything in this life is being divinely guided.

When your loved ones in spirit are trying to connect with you, they will do it in a way that gets your attention. You will start to wonder if it is your loved one or are you making this stuff up? I have come to the realization I am not that gifted to make up this much crap and have it make perfect sense to a sitter during a reading. I have moved beyond my limiting beliefs and concluded I must trust in the information I am being given. With time and practice, you will trust as well. Patience and practice are paramount in developing your gifts.

A final word on synchronicities and meaningful coincidences that appear in your life: Last spring, I met the older gentleman regarding the Cards of Destiny system. He did not randomly show up. It was obvious he was divinely sent to help me. When things like this happen in my life, I sit up and take notice. I do not discount anything as if it happened by coincidence. I am a firm believer that nothing happens without a purpose. So, I studied and learned this system. I had not one but two readings with this system, and in both readings, I was told I had the writer's card present, indicating that I should write, not to mention all the people over the years that have asked me if I would teach what I have learned and write a book.

Six months later, I attended another psychic expo. I gave a lecture titled Channeling 101. At the end of the lecture, I often have people from the audience stop and ask me questions. The last person I spoke with that day handed me her business card and said, "Hi, I work for this company and would like to discuss writing a book for us." Since I had not listened to all the signs, my guides took matters into their own hands and sent the editor to me. I'm telling you all; you can't make this crap up if you tried.

~

Chapter 12:

Putting It Together and Testing for Validation

*"Life becomes way more magical
when you work with the other side."*

– Monica Lawson

The ninth step in the C.O.N.N.E.C.T.E.D. process is Dang I'm Good. In this step, you will be given tips and techniques on how to put together all the previous steps in this process and to test for validation. This step is a recap of everything previously discussed.

You are a spark of the divine. Be confident in your birthright. You have all the spiritual gifts you need in order to connect with the other side. It takes time, patience, and practice. You have learned a lot so far. Now we will put it all together so you can test for results. Remember, you are learning a new language. And your loved ones in the afterlife are working hard to learn how to connect and communicate with you as well. To some extent, they have it a bit easier as they have a clear vision of what is happening on our side of the veil. On the other hand, you can be dense as a doorknob in recognizing the signs, always second-guessing the information and signs you are receiving.

During my development, I was always searching for answers. I have spent most of my life helping others to connect with their loved ones in spirit. At times, it has been heartbreaking, and I have cried right along with my sitter during a reading. At other times, the reading is a blessing. An overwhelming abundance of love flows. The following tips are a culmination of what you learned in the past chapters. Now it is time to put it all together so you can see for yourself how you can connect with your loved ones in spirit and how they are connecting with you.

After some time, you will automatically connect the dots and acknowledge your loved ones and your guides. In the beginning of your development, I highly suggest you keep a daily journal. Write in your journal specific events that you feel may be an odd occurrence. Before going to bed, go over your journal and look back over your day. See if you can make sense of what occurred throughout the day. My husband always says, "Is it odd or is it God?" You can substitute your loved ones in place of God.

Tip #1: No Judgment

Remain non-judgmental in your everyday life when you are interacting with each other. Live a life of harmony and peace always knowing everything is working out for your higher good. Trust in yourself and love yourself. That includes your body and your living conditions. Life is fluid. Nothing is set in stone. Remain flexible with your beliefs. Be willing to look at where and how you developed the beliefs that you are rigid with.

Your relationships and people in your life are your soulmates, your classmates. You agreed to come into this world together to help each other learn, expand, and evolve. Crap happens every day to every person. That is how you and I set the system up. The harder the lesson, the bigger the growth. When life gets difficult, have an open mind and ask yourself, "What is the lesson I am to learn from this?" Then trust the answer will come in one form or another. Do not judge each other. Their path is theirs, and you cannot walk the same path or wear their shoes. Besides, their shoes wouldn't fit anyway.

Tip #2: Spiritual Practices

If you have the desire to connect with your loved ones in the afterlife, you need to set and develop spiritual practices. Have a schedule you follow to meditate and blend with spirit. Once you have a weekly schedule, stick to it. Before long, you will miss it if you do not follow your schedule.

Your thoughts and emotions are an important aspect of your development and growth for your soul. Whenever you experience an extreme emotion, ask yourself, "Is this emotion or thought a reflection of a high vibration or a low vibration?" Then make a shift if it is of a low vibration. You are in control of all your thoughts and emotions. No one has that power over you.

Take a mental inventory of what is feeding your mind every day. I rarely watch TV news anymore. I intentionally do not want to get caught up in that consciousness. Remember, it is how that specific consciousness is trying to suck you into their world, their belief system. If you must watch, then make it a practice to watch a different news media channel every other week until you begin to see how it works energetically from a consciousness vantage point. You will see a difference and probably decide to quit watching every news channel. Or at the least, limit the amount of time you watch. Remember, news channels are set up for doom and gloom. It is the way you are being controlled through fear. If you must watch, pay attention to your emotional state when you first turn on the news, and then check in with your emotional state at the end of watching the news. You will see exactly what I am trying to explain. Can you only imagine how people who have a news channel on all day, every day, are affected? Crazy, isn't it?

Look at your Facebook page, and mentally note what you are looking at on the internet. Do you surround yourself with higher consciousness people? Are you looking and reading feel-good stories, or are you looking at doom and gloom? What you are attracted to is a direct reflection of your inner thoughts and emotions.

Develop affirmations that you read and put into practice daily, even if you say the same one over and over. You are training your mind to believe what you are reading and saying. It takes twenty-one days to form a habit. Stick with the affirmations for a minimum of twenty-one days for that reason. If you easily buy into the news media's daily stories, then you can buy into your affirmations that you wrote.

Tell your friends and family how special they are. Encourage them, inspire them, and pray for them. Every time you send positive vibes to another, it becomes a boomerang and returns to you.

Talk to your loved ones in spirit. They hear every word you say, even if you cannot see them. They have just shed the physical clothing but are still much around you and other loved ones.

Tip #3: Intention and Emotion

Your intention is everything in connecting to your loved ones in the afterlife. Do not be wishy-washy about your desired outcome. Stay positive and know the connection is coming. It is just a matter of time. Then do not waver from that thought of intention.

Remember that sorrow and depression act like a thick cloud, making it difficult to penetrate. The vision always given to me by my guides is when I drive my car in dense fog. I need to slow way down and can only see a few yards in front of my car. This is what grief and depression do. You can still receive information from your loved ones, but it will be slow and sluggish. Work on raising your vibration by remembering the good times, the laughter and the joys.

Imagine how you will feel when you connect with your loved one again. What emotion do you want to convey to them, and what emotion do you wish to feel from them? Your emotions and intentional thoughts create your life and set in motion the law of attraction. You can attract what you desire into your life. Be crystal clear on what the desire is and the outcome you wish. Imagine it, picture it, and feel it.

Set intentions daily. Picture the end-result in your mind's eye. It is like daydreaming. This is good practice and will confirm how powerful your intentions are.

Tip #4: Combine Modalities

I often combine modalities to obtain clarification and confirmation. I have made inquiries using a pendulum and turned right around and used a deck of cards and asked another question regarding the first question in order to validate the first question. I often imagine my spirit guides sitting there shaking their heads because of my lack of confidence. But they oblige me and help me out anyway. Your spirit guides will do the same. I have done the same with numerology, astrology, and Cards of Destiny. I have looked at one system and then turned right around and looked at another system for clarification and validation.

Tip #5: Practice

In order to develop mediumship skills, you also need to develop your psychic abilities and intuition. Practice with friends. Before they tell you what they are doing over the weekend such as household chores, et cetera, take some deep breaths and tune into their energetic field. See what images come to you. Then ask your friend what they are planning to do, or you could wait and ask your friend what they did over the weekend on Sunday evening. See how close you are.

If you are at a restaurant and are waiting for your food, take some deep breaths and then ask yourself how many minutes before the food arrives at my table. Or look at the table next to you and ask how many minutes before they leave the restaurant. I can go on and on, there are lots of questions you can ask and then use your psychic gifts and intuition for the answer. Practice with others, and you will see how fast your development progresses.

I have a lot of fun practicing during movies and TV shows. Whenever there is a movie you are watching in which there is a question of who did it, use your psychic abilities and intuition to tune in and see what you get. You can also do this with any competition show such as the Voice, America's Got Talent, Dancing with The Stars, et cetera. Write your guess on a piece of paper before they announce the winner.

Tip # 6: Water

I was surprised to learn that our bodies are between sixty and seventy percent water. Even our bones contain approximately thirty percent water. Your emotions and thoughts create your everyday reality. Many times, you give it no thought as to when inspiration shows up in your life or when you have an idea for a new project. Start paying attention to how many times during a shower or bath you have a stroke-of-genius thought. Whenever water molecules touch or interact with your body, your emotions and thoughts become heightened. The same can be said for sitting and meditating by a lake, river, or ocean.

Water and our emotions are a great connector to the afterlife. Next time you are in the shower, ask who in spirit is with you today. You will probably be surprised at how fast you get a name. Then use one of the other tips and confirm the name you received.

Tip #7: Playing Cards

Take a regular deck of playing cards and shuffle. Lay the pile face down in front of you. Pick the first card up off the deck, but do not look at it. Lay the card flat on a table by itself and keep your hand or fingers on the card. Imagine if the card is from the red suit or the black suit. Practice, practice, and practice.

Then after some time, remove the court cards. Keep practicing the same way but add the question of what is the card number on the card? This is something you can do on your own. In my experience, I often get bored and the accuracy drops quickly. If you find the same occurs for you, start with ten cards at a time.

Tip #8: Blue or Pink

This is one I use all the time whenever someone is pregnant. I often get asked if someone is having a boy or a girl. I take some deep breaths and ask my spirit guide if they are having a boy or a girl. I wait and see if I am shown pink or blue first. The first color is the color I stick with and is accurate ninety-eight percent of the time. The times it has been incorrect is when the child has a heavy amount of masculine or feminine energy, girls being tomboys or boys being extremely sensitive. Keep this in mind.

This is a fun way to test your abilities and work with your spirit guide as well, especially if you follow this procedure before the parent's test to find out the gender of the baby. It will confirm to you the information you are getting is coming from your guides or your loved ones in the afterlife.

Tip #9: Red Light, Green Light, Yellow Light

Early in my development, I would ask my spirit friends if I should do something. I was asking a yes-or-no question. Immediately, I received flashes of green, red, and occasionally yellow. I knew right away green meant yes. Red meant no, and yellow meant proceed with caution. I still use this in readings all the time. It is easy, and the other side responds quickly.

Tip #10: Pets

I have two dogs. Often, they will alert me when a loved one is near. I will see my dogs looking up in the air with their heads moving as if they are tracking something. Animals are extremely sensitive to energies, smells, and sounds. If you notice this happening with your pets, close your eyes and take a few deep breaths. Then ask, "Who in spirit is here?" The first name that pops into your head is normally correct. You can then confirm this using one of the other tips.

Tip #11: Dreams

There are different types of dreams. It is important for you to understand when your guides are communicating with you through your dreams. It will be a dream you can recall throughout the day and even years later. Your guides do not often enter your dreams, but when they do you will remember it. Keep a dream journal. When you feel you have a profound dream, look up the symbols that appeared in your dream, and you can get a good grasp on what your guides are trying to help you with. Remembering the details such as color, condition of car or building, and numbers is important. Write it down.

Your loved ones will also visit in your dreams. The afterlife is our consciousness. Therefore, they will connect telepathically with you when you are most receptive. Welcome your loved ones into your dreams. Ask them to pay you a visit. If you feel a sense of sadness when you think of them, you are making it difficult for them to enter your dreams. Being receptive and loving is the key.

Tip #12: Symbols

Find a symbol book and stick with that one book. Tell your loved ones and your guides you will use that one book. It makes it much easier for the communication to occur. If you utilize several sources and are inundated with several meanings and interpretations, your guides and loved ones are left with a huge challenge. They will be relieved when you help them and narrow it down to one book.

In searching for a book, there are many dream symbol books and there are many symbol books as well. I use a dream symbol book. I then use the book for both my dreams and my waking life. Once I did this, holy crap, did things change.

Tip #13: Holidays and Celebrations

My mother-in-law passed away in 2016. She was a strong force in our family dynamics. In 2017, while wrapping Christmas gifts, I opened a large gift bag, and at the bottom was a card addressed to my husband and me. The writing seemed familiar to me. I took the card out of the envelope and was surprised to find the card was from my mother-in-law. I was elated. She had found a way to be a part of our holiday celebration. I promptly put her card out on display with all the other Christmas cards and will continue to do so as long as I live.

Any holiday or celebration pay extra close attention to the energies and what is occurring around you. Your loved ones love any and all celebrations. It is a time of love, happiness, and joy. The highest vibrations of all are being demonstrated during celebrations. Because the vibrations are extremely high, your loved ones in spirit can easily ride the wave and often make their presence known.

Tip #14: Oracle Cards

Oracle cards are an easy way to receive guidance and validation from spirit. In my experience, I have found that oracle cards are a tool that can be easily understood by anyone. It does not matter what your level of experience or level of development is. When I was first learning, I would pull an oracle card every day asking, "What does spirit want me to know today?" By doing this, over time, I developed confidence in my abilities, and I learned much about discernment. I found that oracle cards work so well that I currently own over 300 decks. While I enjoy all my decks, I honestly only use approximately three to five decks. I like to think of myself as a collector of oracle cards and various other card systems.

Find a deck that resonates with you. Keep a journal and take notes. Pull a card in the morning. At the end of the day, look at how the card applies to your day. By doing this, you are learning to communicate with the other side and the other side with you.

Tip #15: Music and Sounds

Pay attention to songs that randomly play in your head. Ask yourself who the song is connected to. Pay attention to the words in the song. How do the words apply to your life? If you are sitting and meditating, pay attention to every sound that is occurring around you and within your mind. Be still, and you will start recognizing how the music or sounds fit. Also, pay attention to the songs that play on a radio. If your first thought is a loved one, then the song is definitely coming from them.

Tip #16: Testing Technique for Validation

A few years ago, I was struggling with a decision if I should mentor with a specific medium. It was more money than I had ever paid before. I asked my spirit guides to show me if it was in my highest interest to move forward with the mediumship mentoring. I specifically told my guide to show me three turtles in three days if I should sign up for the mediumship training. Within a few hours, I saw a turtle appear on my Facebook newsfeed. The next day I walked into a clothing store, and there was a shirt with a turtle on the front hanging on a prominent display. But the last thing that occurred was on my way home that evening after my grocery store shopping. I live in the country and need to take the highway and cross the river to get to my home. I was headed home when right before crossing the river bridge, I had to slow down from fifty-five mph to a dead stop on the highway in order to allow a large turtle to cross the highway. The turtle was quite large, approximately thirty pounds. There was no way I could go around the turtle because of a car approaching in the other lane. I had to literally stop. Needless to say, I signed up for mediumship mentoring. It was one of the best decisions I made for my development.

I tell you this story because I came up with the above system in order to know that I am receiving information correctly. You can pick any item you wish. I have used basketballs, roses, chickens, and even turtles. Just remember whatever you pick must be achievable by your loved ones in spirit or your spirit guides. It's not about proving them wrong. It's about giving them an opportunity to work with you and to help you. After making the request, the last thing you need to do is watch for the signs after you state your specific request.

If you wish to connect with your loved ones in spirit, then you must remain open-minded. Being skeptical is fine, and requesting those in spirit to confirm and validate their existence is fine as well. But being stubborn and closed-minded will not get you the results you are hoping to achieve. You must be realistic regarding your questions and demands you place upon those in the afterlife. Remember, even in your life, Superman is fiction.

Tip #17: Effort

You are learning a language that is new to you in some ways. While you have always been receiving signs from the other side, most people let the signs go right over their heads. In order to connect in a way that you receive validation from your loved ones, you must put in the effort and the time to learn and develop. It is like learning to play the piano. With time and effort, you can hone your skills and learn to play the piano well.

Tip #18: Synchronicities

You have often heard people speak of coincidences and synchronicities. I love it when they show up randomly. If you start paying attention to the details that occur every day in your life, you will begin to see them appear everywhere. I had a friend that once posted a saying that said it's important to read between the lines. There is much truth to that. I also tell many people that when you start putting all the synchronicities together, you can't make this much crap up if you tried.

Life is an amazing adventure, an adventure that will reflect to you many clues you can piece together to see who from the afterlife is communicating with you. Take the time to journal and pay attention to the details in your life and the synchronicities that appear. Communication is possible if you use the tips above and the suggestions to test your results. It is a process of observing the details occurring in your life and asking your loved ones in spirit for validation by providing coincidences and synchronicities. Have fun and enjoy the process.

I have listed eighteen of the most popular tips. You will find as you continue to develop there are many more that you could add to the list. Just remember this is all about the experience and learning to put it all together so you can see actual validation. It will help you to build your confidence. Your loved ones in spirit are more than willing to work with you so you do see they are still around. They love you and want to make their presence known. Have fun and keep testing for results. You are much more gifted than you ever realized.

~

Chapter 13:

Love Awaits

*"I look up to the sky and talk to you.
What I wouldn't give to hear you
talk back.
I miss your voice. I miss your laughter. I miss everything about you."*

– Author Unknown

My father passed away in 1986. It is hard to believe it has been thirty-three years since his passing. I miss his hugs and I miss hearing his voice. I would give just about anything to have had a cell phone back then so I could listen to his voice anytime I wanted to today. My children never got to meet their grandfather, and there is a hole in my heart that can never be filled because of that.

I also feel blessed that I had a nudging my entire life to develop my spiritual gifts. I miss my father, my grandparents, and a few friends I have lost over the years, but I also can connect with them, and that brings me a sense of peace. Some days, I even get a good laugh when my dad and grandpa are riding in the backseat of my car talking to each other. I giggle and say, "I can hear that, and why do you both have to ride in the backseat?"

Their thoughts have become so strong I look in the rearview mirror hoping to catch a glimpse of them.

Grief is a scar on your heart. It never completely goes away. And each time you lose a loved one, another scar is added. I once heard a saying that says, "I know the depth of your love by the depth of your pain." How true those words are.

Eventually, you and everyone else will return to your true home, the home where the life of your soul began. There you will rejoin all your loved ones who have journeyed before you. Your loved ones do not die. They just transitioned from one form of being to another. In all reality, they just dropped their physical body, the clothing they wore in this lifetime.

Seeing the Signs

It is my wish for you that by following the steps outlined in this book it will help ease the emotional pain of losing a loved one by teaching you to recognize the signs they are leaving to validate they are still around and much closer than you can ever imagine. The last thing they want is for you to be in pain and have it affect your life. They love you and want you to be happy. Once you can see your loved ones are around, you are able to find joy and happiness again knowing your loved ones interact with you and do see what is occurring in your life. It is an amazing experience when you see for yourself the signs they are leaving. I often refer to it as euphoric.

The more you practice and devote time to meditation and blending with spirit, the easier the connection becomes. It is your birthright and part of your existence as a soul that you are connected to the other side. We are all connected to one another. With just a little guidance, you will see results begin to show up as if by magic. It takes some effort on your part, but I know without a doubt you can do this.

Your Pearl of Great Price

The sad reality is most people have been taught through their beliefs and childhood that the other side should be feared and that if you try to contact the spirit world, it goes against your religion. And yet a large percentage of the population believes that is where we will go after death. And if it isn't your religion that stops you, it may be the fact someone at one time in your life told you to fear the spirit world. How ironic that the person you love so deeply is not in a place you fear.

I remember how difficult it was to step out of the spiritual closet and stand up for what I believed in. It was dang hard, and it took me years to get there. It has been a journey even for me. It is not uncommon if you feel the same way. Most of the population today is keeping their own inner beliefs to themselves for fear of judgment. It may be something that keeps you from moving forward with the process outlined in this book.

In my line of work as a psychic medium, I have spoken to several spiritual seekers with a strong desire to learn and grow. They want to evolve and develop their spiritual gifts and abilities. The problem is they don't know where to start or what steps to follow. For all of you that fit this category, this book is a treasure with lots of tips and techniques. And if you already have a business doing readings, this will be a big benefit in taking it to the next level.

I'm not going to mislead anyone. You will need to put in the effort and practice. I have three grandchildren, and it has been an adventure to watch them learn and experience new things. They think of learning as a fun and exciting time. They never act as if it is difficult or work to try new things. Develop the attitude of wonderment of a child, and you will have much success in putting into practice the C.O.N.N.E.C.T.E.D. process in order to connect with the afterlife. It will be an adventure. And here's a little secret: your loved ones in spirit will love it too. They have been patiently waiting for you to acknowledge them.

I remember when I studied under a well-known mentor. She and I had a long discussion about mediumship and how I felt about it. I explained to her that my mediumship was my own pearl of great price. I could see how valuable it was to everyone it touched. Bringing healing and love to others was the only thing that mattered to me. I had finally learned this lesson well after my phone conversation with Adam's father when he explained to me how my gift of mediumship had given him his wife back. They could now live again and enjoy life. At that moment, I knew every dime I spent was worth its weight in gold. Mediumship is a gift of love. It is my pearl of great price, and perhaps it will become your pearl of great price as well.

The Connected Process

Over the years, I have spent a lot of money getting readings and taking classes only to be disappointed with the outcome. Even some of the international mediums I mentored with did not have an actual process or live up to my expectations. I feel confident you will love this process and find it easy to learn, understand, and implement. It is a small price to pay when it comes to our loved ones.

If you are still reading this book and have made it to the final chapter, I congratulate you on taking the next steps in moving closer to connecting with your loved ones in spirit. In reading this book, you have learned the following process:

C: Courage to See Beyond

You learned why it is important to examine your emotions, beliefs, and thoughts in order to clear the path for connection and how they are directly influencing your life. You were asked to take a closer look at your childhood beliefs and other beliefs you have developed throughout your life and to understand how you came to believe what you do.

O: One with Spirit

Dispelling Myth 1 – Prayer, Protection, and The White Light. You learned why it is not important or necessary for connecting to your loved ones. You will have a clear understanding of why there is nothing to fear. After learning this step, you will view negativity much differently and will change your approach regarding it. To bless someone or something is a much higher vibration than fear.

N: No Judgment

Dispelling Myth 2 – Religion versus Spirituality. You learned that you can combine the two and be at peace. You were introduced to different spiritual practices and the roles our churches play. You now have a better understanding of suicide, purgatory, heaven, and hell. You will also have a clear understanding of how religion and spirituality play a role in just about everyone's life one way or another.

N: No Way, I Can Do This Like the Experts

Dispelling Myth 3 – Medium, Psychic, and Intuitive. You learned how everyone is connected to Source and the afterlife. You learned about soul evolution and spiritual gifts. And you learned the difference between medium, psychic, and intuitive.

E: Education on Mediumship

Mediumship 101. You learned the inconsistencies of mediumship and how to interpret the meaning of each enabling you to work around them. You learned how to determine if the information is coming from a loved one or a guide. You were provided with many development techniques and tips to help you further your development. You learned the nuts and bolts of mediumships and how to interpret certain aspects of mediumship.

C: Commingling Energies

Blending with Spirit. You learned the importance of meditation and meditation techniques. You also learned the difference between meditation and blending with spirit. You learned how implementing each in your daily rituals will help you to connect with your loved ones. You also learned how the spirit world will use your senses to make their presence known to you.

T: The Language of Souls

Soul Language. You learned how your loved ones will communicate with you and you learned the different clairs and how they are used in communication.

This is probably one of the most important steps you will learn throughout the process. You will learn the language itself and see how your loved ones are already speaking to you, but you didn't even realize it.

E: Experience Different Modalities

Tools of the Trade: Divination Systems, Dreams, Numbers, and Synchronicity. You were introduced to a variety of modalities your loved ones will use in order to connect with you. You learned how synchronicity works in communicating with your loved ones. You learned when a visitation dream occurs. And you learned different systems you can use in order to have a clearer connection to your loved ones and guides.

D: Dang I'm Good

Putting It All Together and Testing the Results. In this step, you went back over a recap of many things you learned in the previous steps. You were given examples of how combining the previous steps work together. You also learned testing techniques to get validation from your loved ones in the afterlife. I feel honored and blessed to share this information with you.

My wish for you in writing this book was to provide you clarity about spiritual matters and truths. From the time you were a child, you were taught misconceptions that were not always right and not entirely true. You bought into those teachings. Those misconceptions have been holding you back and blocking your spiritual development. They are delaying your progress.

I want you to move beyond and develop confidence in your understanding of spiritual truths. In doing so, you will have a stable foundation on which to develop your spiritual gifts and abilities.

Eternal Love

I sincerely hope and pray you will learn the process outlined in this book. As with Carol and Jesse, they found much peace and comfort in seeing and recognizing the signs their loved ones were leaving for them. They both took the time and put in the effort to learn, to grow, and to be confident in their abilities. I rarely talk to either one through a reading anymore. I do occasionally receive a message and a description of a sign their loved one has left. It brings a smile to their faces and a sense of peace and a deep love in their heart knowing they are not alone. Their loved ones still see what is happening in their life. It is such a comfort to them.

Carol's life has been extraordinary. She lost her husband and then Daryl a few years later. And yet, when she lost Daryl, she did not suffer the emotional agony or pain she did with her husband. She told me she was at peace with his passing only because she had learned the signs and she could communicate with him immediately. She told me she even giggled at how lively his spirit had become after the suffering of cancer had ended and he transitioned to the afterlife.

I want to reach as many people as possible with this book. I want everyone to have a better understanding of the death process and how the soul lives on well after the physical body has died. My hope is that more people can learn this process and be at peace like Carol. She is an amazing woman that did not stop learning and developing so she could connect herself. She often tells me she experiences and views life much differently than she did before she lost Brian. She is continuing to learn and develop gifts of spirit.

Over the past couple of years, I have gotten to know Brian well. Last week, after writing all but the last two chapters, Carol sent me a picture of her and Brian's headstone. I about fell off my chair when I looked closely at the words written on the headstone. I couldn't believe what I was reading. When I began this book process, I always intended to name Chapter 1 "Love Never Dies." And Chapter 1 was always Carol's story from the beginning. When I looked closely at the fine print in the picture on the headstone, below Carol and Brian's names were the words, "Love Lives Forever." I smiled and thought, Brian, you did it again. I will never stop being amazed at the lengths your loved ones will go through in order to prove a point or get a message to you. Love can move mountains and create miracles. Brian had confirmed to me how important this book is.

This book is for everyone who has given their heart to another. May you find the courage to see beyond the difficulties in putting the C.O.N.N.E.C.T.E.D. process to work in your life. Your loved ones do want to communicate with you. As Brian confirmed, love lives forever.

Blessings to you all.

∼

Acknowledgments

I have wanted to write a book for some time now. I even started numerous times but never seemed to get past the first two chapters. It has been an inner struggle between wanting to help people and yet feeling like I was not good enough. I never wanted to write just any book. If I wrote a book, I wanted to write a book that made a difference.

Several times over the past two years, I have received signs that I was destined to write a book. From psychics telling me, to card readings, to writing being in my chart for the past three years in the Card of Destiny system. It didn't matter how many times it came up, I never felt confident. And to be honest, living in a small town and imagining the gossip about my book did not help boost my confidence.

I always get a chuckle when my spirit friends want to drive a point home. They will do it in such a spectacular fashion that there is no denying the strong suggestion they are making. That's exactly what happened last fall when I was lecturing. At the end of the lecture, an editor from a well-known publishing company approached me about writing a book. I got the point loud and clear from my spirit friends. The problem was I had no idea where to start. I had already tried on my own and was not successful.

Then out of the blue, I had a good friend tell me she was going to write a book with the help of The Author Incubator. She suggested I check it out. So, I did, and I am forever indebted to them. Without the help of the entire Author Incubator team, this book would have more than likely continued for years with me writing chapter one over and over again. Cory Hott, thank you for encouraging me to keep writing forward. Your insight and knowledge during the editing process was priceless. Dr. Angela Lauria, you are brilliant. You have put together a fantastic group of professionals who know their stuff. The experience was magical. Thank you to the entire staff at Author Incubator.

To my faithful followers, thank you for supporting me, attending my lectures, purchasing readings, and giving me a like on my Facebook posts. You are the number one reason this book even exists. It is an honor and privilege to serve you.

To my friends, you all know who you are. I couldn't have done it without you. Your support is the wind beneath my wings. Thank you. I love you all.

To my family, life would not be as sweet without you. You are my joy and reason for getting up every day. I love you to the moon and back.

To my husband, my best friend, and my soulmate, thank you for loving me. I know I have not always made it easy for you. You have always supported me and indulged me in all my whims. I am forever grateful you have been a part of my life for thirty-plus years, and I look forward to growing old with you. I can't imagine life without you. I love you beyond words.

To my spirit friends and loved ones, I hope I have given you all a good laugh from time to time. You have earned it after all I have required of you. You have never let me down and have always been there to pick me up when I couldn't go it alone. Few will ever understand the undeniable connection we share. I am still in such awe and wonderment every single day. I love you. I miss you. Rest in peace, friends; you deserve it.

To those in spirit who are reaching out to connect with your loved ones, this book is for you as well. May your loved ones be led to this book, read it, and put into practice the tips and techniques to see the signs you have been leaving them. I know your desire to heal their broken heart. Don't give up. Keep pushing, and eventually, your hearts will connect again. Namaste.

$\sim$

Thank You!

Thank you so much for reading Death Is Not Goodbye. If you've made it this far, you are well on your way to connecting to your loved ones by putting the C.O.N.N.E.C.T.E.D. process into action.

I would love to hear more about your journey and successes. Please keep in touch. I'm most active on Facebook at "Kim Weaver Evidential Medium and Channel" and on Instagram at @kimweaver.evidentialmedium

For information about my ten-week C.O.N.N.E.C.T.E.D. coaching program, contact me at https://KimWeaverChanneling.com/ or Facebook at Kim Weaver Evidential Medium and Channel via messenger or you can email me at KimWeaverEvidentialMedium@gmail.com

Blessings!

About the Author

Kim Weaver is a psychic medium, spiritual coach, teacher, and speaker who specializes in afterlife communication, spiritual coaching and teaching. She has devoted her life to sharing spiritual wisdom for self-development that empowers others to live a purpose filled life.

Kim has always had a close connection to the spirit world since childhood. Soon after predicting her grandmother's and father's deaths, she began her lifelong study and pursuit of mediumship, psychic development, and several divination modalities. Her certifications include numerology, Lenormand cards, gypsy cards, and psychic detective. Kim has also studied tarot, astrology, Sibilla cards, Le Grand Jeu cards, Human Design, the Gene Keys and the Cards of Destiny.

She has mentored with international mediums in order to further develop her gifts as a mental, trance and physical Medium. As a psychic detective, Kim has helped law enforcement and families locate their missing loved ones.

Grief can impact lives in a profound way after the loss of a family member or friend. It is her mission to help others find the joy and peace of living after the loss of a loved one.

Over the past thirty years, she has noticed an awakening taking place in mass numbers. It is her desire and wish to help others with their spiritual development by sharing her knowledge through personal readings, speaking engagements, mentoring programs, and spiritual coaching.

Kim loves spending time with her family. She lives in Algona, Iowa, with her husband and two dogs.

CPSIA information can be obtained
at www.ICGtesting.com
Printed in the USA
JSHW020754130121
10860JS00004B/174